Pragmatic Vision

LANDMARK PRESIDENTIAL DECISIONS

Series Editor
Michael Nelson

Advisory Board
Meena Bose
Brendan J. Doherty
Richard J. Ellis
Lori Cox Han
James Oakes
Barbara A. Perry
Andrew Rudalevige

Pragmatic Vision

Obama and the Enactment of the Affordable Care Act

Meena Bose

University Press of Kansas

© 2024 by the University Press of Kansas
All rights reserved

Published by the University Press of Kansas (Lawrence, Kansas 66045), which was organized by the Kansas Board of Regents and is operated and funded by Emporia State University, Fort Hays State University, Kansas State University, Pittsburg State University, the University of Kansas, and Wichita State University.

Library of Congress Cataloging-in-Publication Data

Names: Bose, Meena author.
Title: Pragmatic vision : Obama and the enactment of the affordable Care Act / Meena Bose.
Description: Lawrence : University Press of Kansas, 2024. | Series: Landmark presidential decisions | Includes bibliographical references and index.
Identifiers: LCCN 2024000493 (print) | LCCN 2024000494 (ebook)
  ISBN 9780700637430 (cloth)
  ISBN 9780700637447 (paperback)
  ISBN 9780700637454 (ebook)
Subjects: LCSH: United States. Patient Protection and Affordable Care Act. | National health insurance—Law and legislation—United States. | Health insurance—Law and legislation—United States. | Health care reform—United States. | Obama, Barack. | BISAC: POLITICAL SCIENCE / Public Policy / Health Care | POLITICAL SCIENCE / American Government / Executive Branch
Classification: LCC KF3605 .B67 2024 (print) | LCC KF3605 (ebook) | DDC 344.7302/2—dc23/eng/20240710
LC record available at https://lccn.loc.gov/2024000493.
LC ebook record available at https://lccn.loc.gov/2024000494.

British Library Cataloguing-in-Publication Data is available.

For John and Julie Barr
Colin Barr
Lucy Barr
Brian Barr

CONTENTS

Foreword by Brendan J. Doherty ix

Acknowledgments xi

Introduction: Obama's Leadership on Health Care Reform 1

Chapter 1. How Did Health Care Become a Public Policy Priority? 11

Chapter 2. Why Did Obama Make Health Care Reform a Campaign Promise in 2008? 26

Chapter 3. Obama's Early Presidential Leadership and Policymaking Efforts 45

Chapter 4. Obama Succeeds in Enacting the Affordable Care Act 64

Chapter 5. Obama's Health Care Reform Legacy: Implementing and Upholding the ACA 81

Conclusion: Assessing Obama's Leadership 93

Notes 99

Bibliographic Essay 123

Index 129

FOREWORD

The debate over the Affordable Care Act, or Obamacare, as it is popularly known, was at the forefront of American politics for more than a decade, but contentious fights about health care policy go back much further than that. Ever since Harry Truman called for a national health care program in the wake of World War II, presidents have sought to bring the nation closer to that goal. John F. Kennedy advocated for health care for older Americans, and his successor, Lyndon B. Johnson, worked with Congress to create both Medicare and Medicaid in 1965. Jimmy Carter proposed a national health care plan that was not enacted into law. Bill Clinton signed a bill that established the State Children's Health Insurance Program, but his ambitious national health care plan never received a floor vote in either chamber of Congress.

When Barack Obama declared his candidacy for the presidency in 2007, health care became a leading political issue, but recent history offered little hope that efforts to enact comprehensive reform would be successful. After his election in 2008, some counseled the new president to focus on other priorities, but Obama insisted on making health care legislation a key part of his first-year agenda. Health care costs had risen, a smaller percentage of employers were providing health insurance for their workers, and medical-related bankruptcies were devastating many American families.

The fight over health care reform would be fierce, which was unsurprising, given the widely diverging views among elected officials about the government's role in the lives of the American people. What does the common good look like, and what should government do to bring it about? The debate over health care would tap into passionate views of the government's obligation to act to improve the lot of ordinary people, as well as the conflicting belief that individuals have a right be left alone by that same government.

Meena Bose's examination of the enactment of the Affordable Care Act sheds important light on the connections between campaigning and governing, the practical challenges of enacting landmark legislation, the political dynamics of doing so, and the difficulty of implementing substantial new policies. Bose deftly incorporates insights from scholarship on presidential leadership and policymaking as she focuses on eight key decisions Obama made during the 2008 campaign and later as president. The portrait she paints captures the practical political realities of making and implementing policy in a way that highlights not just presidential leadership but also the indispensable role of Congress in the passage of health care reform.

Bose's analysis illuminates a dramatic story marked by many twists and turns: a consequential election, the rare opportunity presented by the Democrats' sixty-vote majority in the Senate, the challenge of building legislative coalitions in both chambers of Congress, the campaign for public support, the death of a key senior senator, an unexpected result in a special election in Massachusetts that shifted the balance of power in the Senate, the use of a procedural tool to get health care over the finish line when many thought reform efforts would fail, the political backlash that followed, and the many challenges of implementing the new law.

Presidents and legislative leaders are remembered for the significant agenda items they accomplish, but descriptions of those achievements are often abbreviated in a way that obscures the complex political landscape they had to navigate to bring their goals to fruition. Readers who are intrigued by the actual ways in which presidents lead will learn much from *Pragmatic Vision: Obama and the Enactment of the Affordable Care Act*. Bose's insightful book brings alive the messy and consequential complexity of presidential-legislative dynamics in play as our leaders work to bring the country closer to their vision of a more perfect union.

Brendan J. Doherty
United States Naval Academy

ACKNOWLEDGMENTS

The mental effort required to write a book truly requires a village of support, and I am fortunate to have so many professional and personal sources of guidance and encouragement. First and foremost, I extend my deepest gratitude to prolific presidency scholar and Rhodes College professor Michael Nelson and University Press of Kansas senior editor David Congdon for developing the Landmark Presidential Decisions series, inviting me to join the editorial board, and welcoming my interest in submitting a proposal. The series makes a unique and important contribution to teaching and scholarship on the modern American presidency, and the dedicated leadership needed to create a new scholarly series is much appreciated. I am especially grateful for Professor Nelson's model of excellence in scholarship, teaching, mentorship, and friendship for more than two decades.

Many of my colleagues in presidency studies, particularly members of the Presidents and Executive Politics (PEP) section of the American Political Science Association (APSA), have shared their expertise on executive leadership and policymaking over the years, and their research has directly or indirectly informed this study. Special thanks to Professor Diane Heith of St. John's University for highly instructive commentary in our 2022 PEP panel and to Professors Dan Ponder of Drury University and Andrew Rudalevige of Bowdoin College for their insights, suggestions, and good cheer about this project during the APSA 2022 conference in Montreal.

The two manuscript reviewers for the University Press of Kansas provided constructive guidance for developing or expanding multiple topics about Obama's key decisions in enacting the Affordable Care Act (ACA), as well as the law's provisions and implementation. To the degree that their recommendations were feasible within the scope of the series, I incorporated them into the book, and it is substantially improved as a result. My deepest thanks to the reviewers for their encouraging assessment and important suggestions for sources and topics.

As I was working on this project, I enjoyed the unique opportunity to direct Hofstra University's Thirteenth Presidential Conference, "The

Barack Obama Presidency—Hope and Change," in April 2023. Building on Hofstra's distinguished tradition since the early 1980s of hosting presidential conferences, the three-day event brought together scholars, journalists, and public officials to conduct a multidisciplinary appraisal of Barack Obama's presidential leadership, policymaking, and legacy. Conference commentary informed my research significantly, and I am grateful to participants for sharing their wealth of knowledge to expand the scholarly record of the Obama presidency. I extend special thanks to Nancy-Ann DeParle, Kate Leone, and Wendell Primus for sharing their firsthand experiences, from executive and legislative perspectives, in the policymaking process that produced the ACA. Their diligence and willingness to share their expertise to inform scholarly studies illustrate the importance and the joys of public service.

I am especially appreciative for the wisdom and guidance of Kalikow Senior Presidential Fellow Philip M. Schiliro (Hofstra class of 1978), who served as director of legislative affairs in the Obama White House during negotiations over the ACA and its passage. He encouraged many public officials to participate in the Hofstra conference and share their recollections of the Obama presidency, particularly in reference to the ACA. Conference participants and the public have a much deeper and richer understanding of the Obama presidency thanks to Schiliro's painstaking efforts and dedication to public service, presidency studies, and Hofstra University. I have learned so much from him about policymaking, and I cherish his friendship. His model of selfless public service is truly inspirational for faculty and students.

Hofstra alumnus Peter S. Kalikow (class of 1965) has generously supported the university's commitment to the interdisciplinary study of the American presidency by creating an endowed chair in presidential studies, an academic center that studies the American presidency, and an interdisciplinary school of government, public policy, and international affairs that examines how institutions and individuals develop public policies. His dedication to democratic leadership and good governance and his genuine enjoyment in learning about the presidency are much appreciated and greatly admired.

Hofstra president Dr. Susan Poser, provost and senior vice president for academic affairs Dr. Charles Riordan, and Hofstra College of Liberal Arts and Sciences dean Dr. Eva Badowska strongly support faculty scholarship and the mission of the Peter S. Kalikow School of Government, Public Policy, and International Affairs and the Peter S. Kalikow Center for the Study of the American Presidency. Their keen interest in research on the presidency that links academic scholarship with practitioner perspectives creates a welcoming environment that encourages scholarly productivity. A special leave from Hofstra to conduct initial research and analysis for the book was essential to its completion and is greatly appreciated.

The Department of Political Science at Hofstra provides a rigorous, nurturing, and collegial community that motivates excellence in teaching and scholarship. Department chair Dr. Carolyn Dudek works tirelessly to promote curricular and scholarly opportunities for students and faculty, steadfastly endorses faculty initiatives, and is a model of academic excellence in teaching, research, service, and academic leadership, as well as a cherished friend. Former dean Dr. Bernard J. Firestone, Dr. Leslie Feldman, and Dr. Rosanna Perotti are mentors and dear friends who have supported and guided my career since I started teaching in 1996. Dr. Craig Burnett is an astute scholar whose rigorous work in American politics, particularly the Kalikow School poll developed at Hofstra for the 2020 presidential election cycle, has produced instructive collaborative scholarship on the presidency that informed this project. Special thanks to Dr. Paul Fritz and Dr. Richard Himelfarb, who served as research director and associate director for the April 2023 conference, respectively. They enriched and expanded my study of the Obama presidency through many wide-ranging and informative conversations, as well as through their dedicated involvement in developing and executing the conference. Dr. Himelfarb generously shared his extensive library on health care policy with me, and our early conversations about this project were highly informative and instructive.

Three students in Hofstra University's Rabinowitz Honors College Undergraduate Research Assistant Program helped me make essential progress in multiple stages of this study. Alexa Paturzo conducted early research for the project and contributed significantly to its conceptual development. Peri Allen prepared multiple annotated bibliographies and biographical summaries for the Obama conference that advanced this project from research to writing. Danny DeCrescenzo painstakingly read every chapter of the manuscript, making thoughtful recommendations that sharpened the analysis and greatly improved the narrative. He also assisted with the development of the bibliographic essay. Sharing the joys of research with these students was rewarding and fun, and I look forward to seeing how their exceptional research, writing, and communication skills advance their own professional development in the coming years. Additionally, students in my American Politics, American Presidency, and Obama Presidency courses bolstered my spirits during research and writing through their continuing enthusiasm for the project. Their keen interest is an encouraging sign for the future of politics and public service and contributed immeasurably to the completion of this book.

Without a doubt, my greatest appreciation goes to my family. My husband, Colin Barr, and our children, Lucy and Brian, bring so much joy, love, and fun to each and every day, and they provided many welcome distractions when research or writing challenges became daunting. We delayed eating dinner or watching a movie countless times until I finished just one more sentence. Lucy famously said that if I was a Barbie, my laptop would be my accessory. I look forward to putting it down to enjoy more family fun, especially our beloved Islanders hockey games!

I dedicated my first book to my parents, sister, and husband; this one is dedicated to my husband, children, and in-laws, John and Julie Barr. Their steadfast love, encouragement, and support over the years have been indispensable and a true joy. Although John passed away in 2022, he knew about this project and always enjoyed talking about the presidency, from his early memories to the present. Bringing this project to completion is a small way of expressing my thanks to everyone mentioned here and to many more dear family, friends, colleagues, and students for sharing this exhilarating academic journey with me.

INTRODUCTION

Obama's Leadership on Health Care Reform

Let's be clear here. Seven presidents have tried to reform a health care system that everyone acknowledges is broken. Seven presidents have failed up until this point.
—President Barack Obama,
60 Minutes interview, 7 December 2009

Some of the same arguments that are made about the Affordable Care Act you heard about Social Security, you heard about Medicare. But once you get over that hump and the thing starts rolling, and people become accustomed to it and confident about it, it ends up helping a lot of people and, you know, that's just the nature of social change in this country.
—President Barack Obama,
Steve Harvey daytime talk show, 20 December 2013

Health care costs are rising at the slowest rate in fifty years. . . . If anyone can put together a plan that is demonstrably better than the improvements we've made to our health care system and that covers nearly as many people at less cost, I will publicly support it.
—President Barack Obama,
farewell address, 10 January 2017

One of President Barack Obama's most significant and enduring policy decisions is signing into law the Patient Protection and Affordable Care Act (ACA) on 23 March 2010. For the first time, the federal government provided every American with the opportunity to obtain guaranteed health care coverage through a system of health insurance exchanges and subsidies to assist with insurance premiums. By expanding the social safety net to include health care, the ACA aimed to ensure that people would not suffer the physical or economic costs of illness by alleviating the burden of finding financially feasible medical care. But the legislative process was highly polarized and contentious, and the law passed on a party-line vote, with almost all Democrats in support and all Republicans opposed. These solid party divisions informed Obama's presidential legacy almost as much as the ACA itself.[1]

In enacting this landmark legislation, Obama achieved a decades-long goal of several of his predecessors. After World War II ended in 1945, President Harry S. Truman called for universal health care as a public right that would "make a most important contribution to freedom from want in our land."[2] Two decades later, Truman witnessed President Lyndon B. Johnson sign into law the historic Medicare and Medicaid programs, which guaranteed access to health care for elderly people (aged sixty-five and older) and low-income earners, respectively.[3] Nearly thirty years later, President William Jefferson Clinton called for universal health care coverage for all Americans.[4] Although Clinton's health care plan did not become law, it provided an important foundation for the legislation the Obama White House endorsed in 2009–10.

Without a doubt, Obama's leadership was essential for passage of the ACA. As a rising politician in the 1990s, Obama had seen the Clinton administration's difficulties in trying to enact health care reform. Before officially launching his presidential campaign in February 2007, Senator Obama (D-IL) announced at a health care policy conference his commitment to ensuring universal access to health care in his first term as president.[5] After prevailing in a pitched battle to win the Democratic presidential nomination and then the White House, Obama insisted on keeping health care at the forefront of his early policy agenda, despite the political risks.[6] He kept his pledge to pass health care reform within four years (doing so in just over fourteen months) and worked closely with Democratic congressional leaders to secure the necessary votes for passage.

To achieve this major policy success, Obama learned from the successes and failures of his predecessors. Since the early twentieth century, the United States had wrestled with the issue of providing health care for all Americans and the government's role in doing so.[7] The Progressive movement, organized labor, and doctors all engaged in policy discussions, but no legislation was passed until the creation of Medicare and Medicaid in 1965. That landmark achievement provided lessons for Obama's policymaking, as did the obstacles the Clinton administration encountered nearly thirty years later.

This book examines how Obama succeeded in enacting the ACA in 2010. Popularly known as Obamacare, the law represents one of Obama's most important achievements. His leadership produced the most significant reform in health care policy in forty-five years, albeit with only Democratic support in Congress. More than a decade later, the ACA continues to be the subject of a defining partisan debate in American politics.

As part of the Landmark Presidential Decisions series, this study evaluates how Obama succeeded in enacting health care reform in the second year of his presidency. Specifically, it focuses on the following key questions: why Obama made health care a campaign issue in 2008; why Obama pursued health care reform early in his presidency; how Obama incorporated concerns from multiple sectors and interests, including the pharmaceutical and insurance industries, to develop the legislation; how Obama employed both public and private strategies to build popular and congressional support; and how Obama addressed various implementation challenges, from early problems signing up for health care plans to court cases that tried to undermine the law's foundations.

Presidential Leadership and Policymaking

In examining Obama's indispensable leadership on the ACA, this study builds on an extensive scholarly literature about the American presidency. A president's views on the responsibilities of White House governance form the foundation of executive leadership. Agenda setting and identification of priorities are essential for making progress toward any major policy decision, and the administration advances the policy process from the executive branch. To enact a law, of course, the legislative and executive branches must work together and build political coalitions in support of the president's priorities. Short summaries of each of these areas of scholarship follow, along with brief applications to the Obama presidency that are more fully developed in subsequent chapters.

Classic studies of presidential leadership focus on the constitutional duties of the office and its evolution. Presidency scholars Edward S. Corwin and Clinton Rossiter examine the creation of the presidency, the components of the executive branch, and the expansion of presidential responsibilities in the modern era, starting in the twentieth century.[8] In the post–World War II era, historians Arthur M. Schlesinger Sr. and Arthur M. Schlesinger Jr. pioneered presidential ratings surveys that considered leadership qualities, with scholars ranking presidents as great, near great, average, below average, or failure.[9] Political scientist Richard E. Neustadt examined presidential leadership through the conceptual lens of the individual in the Oval Office. His classic 1960 study of presidential power presented a model of executive leadership that continues to inform presidency studies in the twenty-first century through its focus on persuasion, a president's professional reputation among Washington elites, and public support.[10] Political scientist Fred I. Greenstein's 2000 study of leadership in the modern presidency provides an enduring guide to internal and external qualities, from cognitive style and emotional intelligence to vision, public communication, organizational capacity, and political skill.[11]

As discussed in chapter 2, Barack Obama's journey to the White House was swift and unexpected, and he was unwavering in his philosophy that executive governance should be grounded in popular participation and engagement in policymaking. Before winning the 2008 presidential race, Obama's previous national political experience had been his work as a first-term US senator from Illinois, elected in 2004. Obama's limited involvement in national politics did not, however, limit his presidential ambitions. In a *New York Times* interview just before he launched his presidential campaign in February 2007, Obama acknowledged that his personality and popular appeal would not be sufficient to win the election. But, he said, "if the campaign is built from the ground up and there is a sense of ownership among people who want to see significant change, then absolutely. It can build and grow." In his campaign announcement, Obama acknowledged a "certain audacity" in his run for president, given that he had not "spent a lot of time learning the ways of Washington." Nevertheless, he declared, "I've been there long enough to know that the ways of Washington must change."[12] Obama promised that his policy platform would reflect public interests by incorporating public involvement throughout the policymaking process—an ambitious and far-reaching goal that was inspirational for his supporters but would not be easy to put into practice.

Presidential scholars have long recognized that after winning the election, presidents-elect must move swiftly to make the machinery of national governance function in their favor. James P. Pfiffner's influential analysis of presidential policymaking discusses the importance of postelection strategic planning in terms of personnel, White House organization, and agenda setting to advance legislative priorities. As Pfiffner writes, "The early actions of a new administration are crucial to its legislative success.... The main legislative accomplishments of an administration are often achieved early in its first year, and... early successes or failures can set the tone for the rest of the administration in its relations with Congress."[13] Paul C. Light's classic study of presidential agenda setting highlights the critical need for priority setting and the skillful use of political capital to make legislative progress.[14]

The smooth and collegial transition from the George W. Bush administration in 2008–9 greatly facilitated Obama's efforts to enter office with an advisory team largely in place and a clearly defined legislative agenda. The nonpartisan Partnership for Public Service praised the "gold standard transition" for its structured and focused coordination between the outgoing and incoming administrations with regard to people, policies, and decision-making processes.[15] Presidential scholar Martha Joynt Kumar notes that when Obama took office, "he had a White House staff structure in place, his personnel office up and running (even if problems persisted), his priorities established, and his initiatives ready to introduce as legislation and executive action."[16] Obama himself thanked President Bush and his administration for "extend[ing] the hand of cooperation and provid[ing] invaluable assistance to my team as we prepare to hit the ground running."[17] Although a smooth transition cannot guarantee legislative success or transformational policymaking, it provides a strong foundation for initial presidential success.

Once in office, presidents require organizational and decision-making structures that adapt to their personal leadership styles *and* provide information, advice, and debate on policy issues. Many scholars have examined how presidents organize the White House staff and executive branch to address policy priorities, daily tasks, and unexpected events or crises.[18] Other scholars approach the topic from a more institutional perspective, analyzing how the office of the presidency creates incentives to centralize policymaking in the White House and make political appointments that will advance the president's agenda.[19] The extensive scholarly literature on presidential leadership style, White House governance, and executive branch policymaking provides important insights into presidential strategies for enacting major policy overhauls.[20]

Consistent with his presidential campaign and the transition period, Obama adopted a structured and carefully organized White House decision-making process. Six of his fifteen cabinet nominees were confirmed on Inauguration Day, and several more followed in the next week. Two positions—secretaries of commerce and health and human services—were not filled until spring.[21]

Obama employed a deliberative decision-making style that could take time, and he actively participated in policy discussions. As Pfiffner writes, Obama "require[ed] his staffers to argue their cases in front of him. . . . Perhaps the most striking characteristic of Obama's decision-making style was his personal involvement in the details of policy." Pfiffner concludes: "President Obama conducted the type of decision-making processes often advocated by political scientists. Obama's approach guaranteed that he fully examined all serious policy options. Whether or not he made wise decisions is a separate issue."[22]

The academic fields of presidency studies and policy studies have produced many scholarly sources on the policymaking process between the White House and Congress. As discussed earlier, Neustadt's classic study of presidential power focuses on how presidents exercise leadership through persuasion and bargaining. Subsequent studies place Neustadt's model of individual action in an institutional context, examining how White House and executive branch staff as well as members of Congress can guide or constrain executive actions.[23] The literature on policymaking examines how multiple policy ideas and proposals coalesce into a specific plan of action when political timing, actors, and opportunities come together. Political scientist John Kingdon presents a persuasive conceptual policymaking model that focuses on the convergence of three "streams": problem identification, political conditions, and policy options. In the presence of broad consensus on problem identification, favorable political conditions, and workable policy options, prospects for policy enactment are highly favorable.[24]

A combination of assertive presidential leadership and party control of Congress resulted in passage of the ACA. Following through on his campaign promise, Obama made health care reform the centerpiece of his domestic policy agenda in 2009, despite many other pressing priorities, most notably the Great Recession that started in late 2007 and continued into 2009, after which the United States experienced a long, slow path to economic recovery.[25] Additionally, Obama benefited from the convergence of the three streams in Kingdon's conceptual model of US policymaking. As Kingdon writes, "With all three streams joined, fundamental health reform had a good chance during 2009 and 2010, and we know a lot more about why President Obama succeeded and President Clinton and all of his predecessors did not."[26]

Even with passage of the ACA, Obama faced public ambivalence about the law, which represented an underlying ideological debate about the federal government's role in health care and the limits of presidential leadership in shaping public opinion. A March 2010 Gallup poll found that 50 percent of the public was "enthusiastic" or "pleased" about the ACA, 41 percent were "disappointed" or "angry," and 8 percent had no opinion.[27] This division brought into sharp relief an inherent contradiction in the office of the presidency: the public often has high expectations of bold and visionary executive leadership, but it still wants presidents to act within the broad contours of popular support.[28] Presidents themselves may want to guide public opinion, but in practice, they have limited ability to influence public attitudes. Presidential scholar James MacGregor Burns theorizes that political leaders often aspire to achieve "transformational" change that will steer followers in new directions to advance the public good. As Burns explains, "the transforming leader recognizes and exploits an existing need or demand of a potential follower."[29] In contrast, "transactional" leadership focuses on the typical political processes of negotiation, bargaining, and compromise. Transactional leadership is much more common, but transformational leadership can be far more consequential yet very difficult to achieve.

Well before he ran for president, Obama expressed interest in transformational leadership. As a US senator hinting at a possible White House campaign, he noted that presidents "want to change the country. You want to make a unique contribution. You want to be a great president."[30] Weeks before the 2008 general election, Obama defined "great presidents" as "those who transform how we think about ourselves as a country . . . they transformed the culture and not simply promoted one or two particular issues."[31] But changing the culture and people's thinking typically requires drastic circumstances, such as a political or economic crisis, to even present the possibility of achieving an enduring shift in public opinion.

Without a doubt, Obama's actions as president moved health care reform forward at several points when the obstacles seemed insurmountable.[32] Other officials and advisers played critical roles in the policymaking process, but Obama's steady and persistent leadership grounded the political battles. Furthermore, Obama remained steadfast in supporting health care reform despite strong public criticism and electoral complications, even declaring that he "would rather be a really good one-term president than a mediocre two-term president."[33] Still, Obama's inability to shift public opinion about the ACA may illustrate what political scientist and psychoanalyst Stanley Renshon describes as "transformational ambitions, but not transformational circumstances."[34]

Landmark Decisions Leading to Enactment of the ACA

To examine the policymaking stages that led to passage of the ACA, this study begins with a brief overview of the evolution of health care policy in the United States. In particular, it examines Truman's call for universal health care after World War II, Johnson's creation of Medicare and Medicaid, and Clinton's efforts to expand access to health care. The study then focuses on Obama's leadership in health care reform from the 2008 presidential campaign to early administration debates about prioritizing access to health care for all Americans. After analyzing how Obama's decisions influenced the major institutional and political actors responsible for passage of the ACA, this study examines Obama's ongoing leadership in implementing and defending the law.

In addition to highlighting the importance of presidential leadership for policymaking, examining how Obama prioritized health care reform and the ACA is instructive for understanding executive agenda setting and decision making.[35] This case study illustrates prospects for twenty-first-century presidential leadership, as well as the challenges of overcoming institutional obstacles to policy action in the American political system.

Examining how Obama navigated the highly partisan policymaking process that produced the ACA also informs scholarly research on party politics and American democratic governance in the twenty-first century. Since the late 1990s, American politics has become increasingly polarized, with sharply pronounced ideological differences between the Democratic and Republican Parties that permit little, if any, opportunity for negotiation, bargaining, and compromise.[36] Political scientists have examined many aspects of polarization, such as whether today's zero-sum policy divisions are confined largely to political elites or are present in the general public as well, and whether polarization is grounded in individuals' policy views or has become more intrinsic to Americans' social identity.[37] This study evaluates how Obama directed public and legislative debates about the ACA and how party polarization shaped those debates.

In examining Obama's leadership in enacting the ACA, eight landmark decisions are evident:

1. Make a firm commitment to health care reform in the 2008 presidential campaign.

2. Identify health care reform as an immediate priority in 2009.

3. Exercise White House leadership to start the policymaking process for health care reform in the spring of 2009.

4. Defer to Congress to develop health care legislation in the summer of 2009.

5. Refocus legislative efforts on health care reform in the fall of 2009.

6. Continue to advance health care reform after the Democrats lose their filibuster-proof Senate majority in January 2010.

7. Enact the ACA through the budgetary process of reconciliation in March 2010.

8. Allow flexibility in implementing the ACA following court rulings and initial technical hurdles.

These decisions are examined in chapters 2–5.

Chapter 1 presents the major legislative efforts and achievements that preceded the Obama presidency in the Truman, Johnson, and Clinton administrations. Chapter 2 examines Obama's decision to make health care reform a signature issue of his 2008 presidential campaign. Chapter 3 examines Obama's leadership on health care reform in 2009, including making the issue a legislative priority, initiating reform discussions at the White House, deferring to Congress on the initial development of legislation, reseizing the initiative to draft legislation, and working closely with legislators to ensure that the House and Senate passed reform bills before year's end. Chapter 4 examines Obama's success in enacting the ACA in 2010 through a revised legislative strategy following the Democrats' loss of a filibuster-proof Senate majority. Chapter 5 examines the enduring achievements of the ACA, despite initial bureaucratic hurdles and judicial challenges. The conclusion assesses Obama's leadership in navigating health care reform, as well as the challenges of navigating political support and opposition in Congress and public opinion to bring a pragmatic policy vision to fruition.

CHAPTER 1

How Did Health Care Become a Public Policy Priority?

We should resolve now that the health of this Nation is a national concern; that financial barriers in the way of attaining health should be removed; that the health of all its citizens deserves the help of all the Nation.
—President Harry S. Truman,
"Special Message to the Congress Recommending a Comprehensive Health Program," 19 November 1945

No longer will older Americans be denied the healing miracle of modern medicine. . . . And no longer will this Nation refuse the hand of justice to those who have given a lifetime of service and wisdom and labor to the progress of this progressive country.
—President Lyndon B. Johnson,
"Remarks with President Truman at the Signing in Independence of the Medicare Bill," 30 July 1965

At long last, after decades of false starts, we must make this our most urgent priority, giving every American health security, health care that can never be taken away, health care that is always there.
—President William J. Clinton,
"Address to a Joint Session of Congress on Health Care Reform," 22 September 1993

President Obama's focus on health care reform was grounded in decades of US policy planning, accomplishments, and disappointments. The United States developed national social welfare programs much later than other industrialized democracies for multiple reasons, including the founding principles of limited government and federalism. Still, by the early twentieth century, increased life expectancy and advances in medical technology created opportunities for hospital and physician care that extended far beyond the treatment of fatal illnesses.[1] As a result, health insurance plans were developed, particularly for workers who were insured through businesses and labor unions.

This chapter presents an overview of the evolution of health care policy in the United States, with special attention to the three presidents who influenced Obama's policy agenda and decision making on health care reform: Harry S. Truman, Lyndon B. Johnson, and William J. Clinton. Each president's legislative goals, achievements, and difficulties were highly instructive for the Obama administration's success in enacting the Affordable Care Act.

The Evolution of US Health Care

In the United States, social policy has historically been the primary focus of states and nonprofit organizations. In other advanced industrial democracies, the national government typically oversees such programs, and health care is no exception. US efforts to establish health care in the public sphere date to the nineteenth century, starting with the collection of data on health conditions in communities. In the early twentieth century, the Progressive movement, which worked to improve society by regulating business, fighting corruption in government, and expanding democratic participation, advocated strongly for public health care.[2] But public officials largely criticized proposals to have the federal government manage health care, and US involvement in World Wars I and II sharply constrained policy possibilities.[3]

Following the western European model, US scholars started collecting data on public health problems in the 1830s to guide policy decisions. The creation of the American Public Health Association in 1872 led to the dissemination of surveys to towns with populations exceeding five thousand to collect information on community health topics such as water supply and building ventilation.[4] In the early twentieth century, groups that shared the Progressive movement's goals of making government more responsive to people's needs called for health insurance to assist individuals obtain medical care and maintain income during illness. The American Association for Labor Legislation promoted mandatory health insurance such as that provided in England and Germany, which covered sick pay as well as payments to hospitals and physicians. The American Federation of Labor (AFL) advocated union organizing to negotiate with employers.[5]

In 1912 former president Theodore Roosevelt made a public commitment to health care when he campaigned for the White House as a candidate for the Progressive Party, whose platform endorsed health insurance.[6] The Socialist Party had done the same in its 1904, 1908, and 1912 platforms, but Roosevelt's candidacy, albeit unsuccessful, brought more visibility to the issue. The American Association for Labor Legislation subsequently drafted proposed legislation for health insurance, which the American Medical Association (AMA) endorsed, and it lobbied for mandatory health insurance in eight states. With the start of World War I, however, support for health care reform diminished. The AMA changed its position, now opposing mandatory insurance primarily because of concerns by state chapters that it might result in lower wages.[7] The Progressive movement continued to support public health care guarantees, including lower medical costs, expanded access to care, and sick leave for workers, with officials in both the Republican and Democratic Parties endorsing these reforms.[8]

Economic hardship and widespread suffering during the Great Depression prompted a resurgence of interest in health insurance, although policymaking stalled in the face of opposition to a national program. In the 1930s Democrat Franklin Delano Roosevelt supported medical coverage early in his presidency, but opposition from the AMA halted those plans. Another organization of physicians and academics, the Committee on the Costs of Medical Care, had formed in the 1920s to advocate for health care reform, but members who served in FDR's administration were unable to build popular support for its proposals. The AMA's critique of the committee's call for public health insurance as "socialized medicine" dominated the policy debate and sidelined the issue through World War II.[9] Only after the war would health care receive prominent presidential backing.

Truman Endorses Public Health Care

Harry Truman was the first president to call for a public guarantee of access to health care. He declared his commitment to a federal policy early in his presidency (taking office on 12 April 1945 after the shocking death of FDR) and in his 1948 presidential campaign, but Cold War politics and charges of socialism, as well as other domestic priorities, were insurmountable obstacles after World War II. Interest groups such as the AMA galvanized opposition to government-run medical care, and the White House did not devote political capital to overcoming these obstacles. Still, by placing public health care on the broad policy agenda, Truman ensured that subsequent administrations would continue to press forward with these efforts.

Within a year of taking office, Truman expressed public support for a national health care policy. On 7 November 1945 he devoted an entire special message to Congress to health care, expanding on a September message calling for an Economic Bill of Rights that included medical care, good health, and protection from economic loss during sickness. In his November message, Truman declared that the nation's health was a national concern. Guaranteeing health care for all Americans, Truman said, would "make a most important contribution toward freedom from want in our land."[10] In a January 1946 radio address, Truman encouraged Congress to take action in multiple policy areas to improve economic conditions, including health and medical care, and he reiterated this point in public statements throughout his presidency.[11] The Democratic Party bolstered Truman's stance by endorsing "enactment of a national health program" in its 1948 platform, which Truman advocated as the party's nominee.[12]

Still, following through on this priority required congressional support, which Truman lacked in his almost eight years as president. After World War II ended, Truman faced the difficult task of fulfilling the public's deep desire to enjoy peacetime conditions while dealing with ongoing economic challenges. Food shortages, limited access to material goods, labor conflicts, and inflation all hurt Truman's approval rating, and every decision he made, whether well thought out or impulsive, inevitably led to unfavorable comparisons with FDR's leadership. The 1946 midterm elections were a referendum on Truman's presidency, with disappointing results for him as Republicans took control of both chambers of Congress, winning their largest number of House seats in more than fifty years.[13] Two years later, Truman won the presidential race in a stunning upset, and the Democrats regained control of Congress. They kept control in 1950, albeit by a smaller margin. But the Korean War, which had started earlier that year, dominated the rest of Truman's presidency, resulting in his decision not to run for reelection in 1952, even though he was eligible to do so, as he was not bound by the two-term limit of the recently ratified Twenty-Second Amendment. This pushed aside important but distant policy goals such as national health care.

Further complicating policymaking in this area was the start of the Cold War and associated critiques of government programs as "socialism." The AMA had opposed national health care for the last three decades, insisting that a government-mandated program would lead to higher costs and lower quality of care.[14] Furthermore, the AMA warned that diverting resources from waging the Cold War would be detrimental to the United States. As one author explains, "The AMA used rhetoric of the anti-communist movement in the United States at the time to warn against social democracy—which was just one step away from communism in their view."[15]

An unexpected ascension to the presidency, the transition to a post–World War II economy, high unpopularity for extended periods, and the Korean War gave Truman little time for major policy overhauls during his nearly two terms in office. Although he expressed support for a national health care program multiple times, Truman did not devote any political capital to advancing a legislative proposal. Given the many domestic, economic, and foreign policy challenges he faced as president, this was not surprising.

The dawn of the Cold War and related fears that any government-run program would bring socialism to the United States hindered prospects for health care reform, as did the staunch opposition of the AMA and other organized interests in the medical field. But Truman's public commitment to a national health care program provided a good foundation and a clear direction for his successors to pursue in more promising times.

Johnson Enacts Medicare and Medicaid

A decade after Truman left office, Lyndon Johnson also moved from the vice presidency to the presidency, but in far more trying circumstances after the shocking assassination of President John F. Kennedy on 22 November 1963. (Although FDR's passing stunned the nation and sparked worldwide mourning, his death was due to poor health.) Unlike Truman, Johnson had waged a presidential campaign of his own, and he became Kennedy's running mate in 1960 due to his ability to balance the ticket geographically. As a native of Texas, Johnson provided a good contrast to Kennedy's Massachusetts roots. Furthermore, Johnson was an experienced legislator who had served in both the House and the Senate, including several years as Senate majority leader. Although Johnson's elevation to the presidency was unexpected, once he took office, he was well prepared to advance Kennedy's policy proposals as well as long-standing Democratic goals such as health care reform. Less than two years into his presidency, Johnson signed the historic legislation that guaranteed national health care for elderly and low-income Americans.

In a special message to Congress on 27 November 1963, Johnson affirmed his commitment to enacting an ambitious agenda that would enshrine Kennedy's legacy in American politics. Highlighting Kennedy's goals of space exploration, an active Peace Corps to promote development worldwide, access to education and jobs, and, most importantly, equal rights for all Americans regardless of skin color, Johnson promised to act swiftly in each area. Above all, Johnson emphasized the critical need for civil rights legislation, famously declaring, "We have talked long enough in this country about civil rights. We have talked for one hundred years or more. It is time now to write the next chapter, and to write it in the books of law." Johnson did not address health care specifically, but he did refer to "the dream of care for our elderly—the dream of an all-out attack on mental illness."[16] Less than two months later, Johnson delivered his first State of the Union address to Congress and called on legislators to make 1964 "the session which finally recognized the health needs of all our older citizens."[17]

In seeking to enact health care reform, Johnson faced obstacles similar to those Kennedy experienced. In 1962 Kennedy actively pressed for health care for the elderly, seeking to build public momentum with union support from the AFL-CIO. While union members organized rallies around the country, Kennedy delivered a major address on health care at New York City's Madison Square Garden on 20 May 1962.[18] Speaking to a full house of almost twenty thousand people, Kennedy vividly illustrated how illness could devastate a family financially due to the high cost of health care. He gave multiple examples and cited the hospital care his father had received (and could afford) as a model for what should be available to all older Americans. Describing the lack of guaranteed medical care for the elderly as "a great national crisis," Kennedy called on people to petition their elected officials for change.[19] But this public strategy foundered in the face of vehement opposition from physicians and the medical industry.

Ever since passage of the Social Security Act in 1935, guaranteeing income for the elderly, public health advocates had pressed for guaranteed medical care for the elderly. Opponents insisted that a government-run program would infringe on physicians' ability to make medical decisions, restrict innovations in medical research, and sacrifice high-quality health care. As Ronald Reagan said as a spokesman for General Electric in 1961, a failure to oppose "socialized medicine" would mean that "you and I are going to spend our sunset years telling our children, and our children's children, what it once was like in America when men were free."[20] But Johnson's landslide victory in the 1964 presidential election, combined with Democratic gains in Congress, provided a window of opportunity for policy action.[21]

Johnson's vision of a Great Society included health care for the elderly. In his address to Congress on 4 January 1965 (the first State of the Union message televised in prime time), the president advocated "providing hospital care [to the elderly] under social security."[22] Johnson had endorsed a provision that added hospital insurance for the elderly to Social Security legislation in 1964. It passed by a vote of forty-nine to forty-four in the Senate but was blocked in the House by Wilbur Mills (D-AR), who chaired the Ways and Means Committee. The coalition of Republicans and southern Democrats that opposed Medicare weakened after the 1964 elections, when Democrats gained thirty-six seats in the House and retained their two-thirds majority in the Senate.[23] Now that Democrats had the votes to pass Medicare legislation, private White House negotiations with Mills (which included the president's assurance that he would get credit for the program) convinced the congressman to become an advocate for health care reform. Mills even proposed broader legislation that included physician and hospital insurance for the elderly as well as medical assistance for the poor (building on a proposal he had cosponsored a few years previously for federally funded and state-run medical assistance for indigent elderly Americans).[24]

Ultimately, both Democrats and Republicans in Congress voted for the bill, albeit with much greater Democratic support (there was some Democratic opposition in both chambers as well, although Republicans were more strongly opposed).[25] On 30 July 1965 Johnson signed legislation to create Medicare and Medicaid (formally the Social Security Amendments of 1965—Title XVIII of the Social Security Act for Medicare and Title XIX for Medicaid). He did so in Independence, Missouri, with former president Truman seated next to him. Truman then became the first person to enroll in Medicare, and he and his wife, Bess, received the first Medicare insurance cards.[26]

Johnson's skillful negotiations with Mills were critical to the creation of Medicare and Medicaid, as was a favorable political environment in Congress.[27] Repeated efforts and disappointments over the past thirty years had paved the way for action in 1965, and in some respects, the president achieved more than he had originally hoped for by providing access to health care for two groups who desperately needed it. Still, this landmark legislation fell short of Truman's call for guaranteed access to health care for all Americans. Despite multiple efforts by subsequent presidents to expand health care coverage and lower costs, nearly thirty years passed before the next major presidential initiative to achieve universal health care coverage in the United States.[28]

Clinton Tries to Reform Health Care

Bill Clinton's successful presidential campaign in 1992 marked both a generational change in American politics and a major shift in US policy priorities. Clinton's predecessor, George H. W. Bush, had presided over the end of the Cold War after serving as vice president for eight years during the transformation of US-Soviet relations in the 1980s. Bush, a World War II veteran, had focused on foreign policy as president, and during his 1992 reelection campaign he pledged to pay more attention to domestic policy in his second term. Clinton, who had opposed the Vietnam War in college and afterward, made personal connections with the public, acknowledging people's economic problems and highlighting their need for jobs and security so they could pursue their personal goals.

Health care was a key component of that security, and Clinton won the White House by promising economic growth and greater access to medical services. The economic recession of the early 1990s and slow job growth, combined with the soaring cost of health insurance premiums, made calls for health care reform more visible and compelling to voters.[29] Clinton's victory heralded the possibility of transformational change in domestic policy, perhaps making Truman's vision of guaranteed health care a reality for all Americans.

Less than two years after taking office, however, Clinton was forced to defer his ambitious plans. His failure to fulfill this campaign promise was grounded in multiple factors. First, although health care was important to Clinton, it was not his top policy goal; his priority was to revitalize the US economy through deficit reduction and expanded job opportunities. Second, upon taking office, Clinton created a task force to develop a health care plan, and he asked his wife, Hillary Rodham Clinton, to lead it. Putting the First Lady in charge of one of the administration's signature policy issues clearly illustrated its importance. However, the president's decision also made criticizing or raising concerns about the task force's work difficult, which, combined with the secrecy surrounding the process, hindered progress. Third, Clinton was not attentive to disagreements within the Democratic Party about the best path forward with regard to health care, and those conflicts hampered his efforts to build legislative support. Fourth, the complexity of the administration's thousand-plus-page plan mobilized opposition among interest groups and within Congress in the fall of 1993. Ultimately, Clinton's plan was so unpopular that it never came to a full congressional vote in 1994. Instead, Clinton enacted modest health care reform in 1996, leaving a broader overhaul to subsequent administrations.

From the start of his presidential campaign in late 1991, Clinton's primary focus was the economy. Announcing his candidacy from the Old State House in Little Rock, Arkansas, where he had recently won election to a third term as governor, Clinton promised to fight for much-needed change to ensure a brighter American future.[30] As he stated: "I refuse to be part of a generation that celebrates the death of Communism abroad with the loss of the American Dream at home. I refuse to be part of a generation that fails to compete in the global economy and so condemns hard-working Americans to a life of struggle without reward or security." Clinton also pledged to improve health care, declaring, "Opportunity for all means reforming the health care system to control costs, improve quality, expand preventive and long-term care, maintain consumer choice, and cover everybody."[31] Nevertheless, although health care was a key component of the American Dream, Clinton campaigned mostly on economic issues. This was vividly illustrated by the slogan used by chief strategist James Carville to motivate campaign workers: "It's the economy, stupid."[32]

Within a week of taking office in 1993, President Clinton announced the creation of the Task Force on National Health Care Reform, as well as the White House Health Care Interdepartmental Working Group. First Lady Hillary Clinton would lead the twelve-member task force (which included several cabinet secretaries) in preparing a comprehensive health care reform plan for the administration. The working group would be headed by White House senior domestic policy adviser Ira Magaziner, a business consultant and close friend of the president's since they attended Oxford University as Rhodes scholars in the late 1960s. This group was responsible for conducting research on previous health care reform initiatives, policy options, examples from state and international programs, and other topics to assist the task force, which would draft a legislative proposal in the first hundred days of the administration.[33] Group members included more than five hundred participants from the public and private sectors, such as federal and state agencies, congressional offices, nonprofit organizations, health care professionals, and policy activists.[34] The Clinton administration initially refused to release a list of working group members but ultimately did so two months later, after many names had already been leaked to the media.[35]

Secrecy was one of many problems the task force faced, but perhaps the most complicated was having the First Lady in charge. Like her husband, Hillary Clinton had been a rising star from a young age. She was featured in *Life* magazine in 1969 for being the first student to deliver a graduation speech at Wellesley College (Magaziner was featured in the same issue as valedictorian from Brown University). She subsequently excelled at Yale Law School (where she met Bill Clinton), served on the congressional staff during the presidential impeachment inquiry resulting from the Watergate scandal, and then joined the prestigious Rose Law Firm in Little Rock after moving there and marrying Clinton.[36]

In another administration, Hillary Clinton would have been a logical choice for a senior position, but in her husband's administration, blending personal ties with a high-profile policy initiative was problematic. People were reluctant to raise concerns about the task force with the president, and the initial effort to maintain secrecy demonstrated an unfamiliarity with how Washington functions. Several groups filed a lawsuit demanding that the task force proceed in public, as required by the 1972 Federal Advisory Committee Act for government panels with private individuals as members, which, the plaintiffs claimed, included the First Lady. A federal appeals court ultimately ruled in favor of the administration, stating that the First Lady qualified as a government official, albeit with ambiguous authority, and that the president must be able to receive confidential advice. By this time, the task force had completed its work, but the difficulty of having the First Lady direct the process was clear.[37] As one senior adviser later wrote, "The President, without meaning to, gave the First Lady 'mission impossible.'"[38]

Through the spring and summer of 1993 the Clinton administration prepared its comprehensive proposal for health care reform. The multiple subunits of the working group examined numerous aspects of the health care system, including size, complexity, and benefits packages. But the White House was focused on deficit reduction, and the task force lacked leadership with national legislative expertise. Two policy scholars noted, "Some experienced hill staffers, came to the conclusion that the task force was really about educating Magaziner, Mrs. Clinton, and their inner circle about the basics of writing national health insurance legislation."[39] The White House dissolved the task force in May, and once the budget passed on a party-line vote in August, the president's staff turned their full attention to developing a health care plan.

By early fall, the administration was ready to present its proposal publicly. On 22 September 1993 President Clinton delivered an address before Congress explaining his ambitious agenda for health care reform. Despite a problem with the teleprompter (because the final speech was unavailable earlier in the day to test the machine, a different speech had been uploaded), Clinton skillfully spoke extemporaneously and from the printed text for several minutes until the correct words appeared onscreen. Calling for monumental policy change, Clinton declared that every American should have health security. Holding up a sample card, the president said, "Under our plan every American would receive a health care security card that will guarantee a comprehensive package of benefits over the course of an entire lifetime roughly comparable to the benefit package offered by most Fortune 500 companies."[40] Days later, Hillary Clinton became the third First Lady (after Eleanor Roosevelt and Rosalynn Carter) to testify before Congress, speaking for four hours to the Ways and Means Committee and the Energy and Commerce Committee to explain the health care plan's rationale and feasibility.[41] The administration subsequently sent a voluminous legislative proposal of more than thirteen hundred pages to Congress for deliberation and decision making.[42]

As indicated by its length, the health care bill was a highly complex and layered program that presented multiple opportunities to identify its shortcomings. The Health Insurance Association of America (HIAA) and the National Federation of Independent Business were highly critical of proposals to regulate insurance premiums, limit plan choices through managed competition, and establish an employer mandate for health insurance. The HIAA highlighted public concerns about the bill's complexity and cost through its famous "Harry and Louise" ads, which showed a couple sitting at the kitchen table expressing their worries about losing access to existing coverage options. As Louise said, "Having choices we don't like is no choice at all." To which Harry replied, "If they choose, we lose."[43] Put on the defensive, the Clinton administration lacked clear and concise responses to these critiques. Part of the problem was that neither of the Clintons had expertise in Washington policymaking and dismissed recommendations for compromise or more incremental reform. The decision-making process lacked structure, and Hillary Clinton's leadership style did not encourage constructive debate. According to Washington journalist Elizabeth Drew, who interviewed many of the key White House and congressional participants, some people who worked with Hillary "found her intimidating—hard to argue with and uninterested in the points they made."[44]

President Clinton's efforts to navigate the obstacles to enacting monumental health care reform were ultimately unsuccessful. In his January 1994 State of the Union address, Clinton made the surprising announcement that he would veto legislation that did not guarantee health insurance for all Americans. This position blocked the possibility of building a coalition with moderate Democrats who endorsed parts of Clinton's managed competition plan but were reluctant to approve an employer mandate. As a result, the Clinton White House lacked sufficient support within the Democratic Party to move forward and faced strong Republican opposition as well. The inability to negotiate for congressional votes, combined with Clinton's declining public approval rating (due to multiple policy, organizational, and image problems), jeopardized prospects for health care reform, and by mid-1994 the effort had stalled, without a vote in either chamber of Congress.[45]

Halfway through Clinton's term, his presidency appeared to be moving toward a disappointing end in two more years as high ambitions gave way to harsh political realities that also hurt the president's political party. The 1994 midterm elections had devastating results for Democrats, who lost control of the House for the first time in forty years and of the Senate for almost the same period (apart from six years of Republican Senate control from 1981 to 1987). Republican leadership in Congress dominated the policy agenda by advocating a Contract with America that would balance the budget, cut taxes, impose congressional term limits, and retool several social welfare programs.[46]

In April 1995 only one television network carried a live broadcast of the president's first prime-time news conference in eight months, and Clinton insisted that he could still influence policymaking because "the Constitution gives me relevance."[47] Then the Republicans overreached, prompting two government shutdowns in 1995–96 because Clinton refused to approve their budget proposals, which he said imposed draconian spending cuts that would hurt Americans.[48] Clinton prevailed in this showdown and went on to win reelection easily in 1996. Shortly before the election, he even succeeded in enacting health insurance portability, which guaranteed that individuals could keep their health insurance if they changed jobs, although they would be responsible for paying the premiums.[49] In his second term, Clinton signed the State Children's Health Insurance Program (SCHIP), which increased federal funding to states to provide health care coverage for children whose parents earned more than the maximum threshold for Medicaid but not enough to purchase family health insurance.[50]

The ambitious scope of Clinton's initial health care reform plan and a more restrictive political environment than originally perceived, as well as leadership mistakes, explain the failure of the president's signature domestic policy priority. Despite Clinton's solid election victory and Democratic control of Congress, the White House lacked both legislative and public momentum for a major health care overhaul.[51] According to former Clinton White House adviser David Gergen, the president was more focused on his economic and trade agenda than on health care, but because his wife was leading the health care reform mission, he felt obligated to press forward, despite her lack of legislative expertise.[52] Responsibility for the policy failure ultimately rests with the president, of course, and Clinton failed to acknowledge political realities or heed criticisms of his organizational choices.[53] In retrospect, the president viewed competing expectations for health care coverage and cost as the primary problem, along with the White House strategy for drafting legislation; he insisted that Hillary Clinton's leadership on a thorny issue had been sound.[54] As he later told a journalist, "It was my mistake, not hers. All she did was what she was asked to do. . . . Health care was all my fault."[55]

Conclusion

The evolution of US health care policy in the twentieth century presented many lessons, both positive and cautionary, for President Obama. Truman's vocal commitment to guaranteed health care for all Americans established a long-term goal for his successors to pursue. Johnson's success in enacting health care for elderly and low-income individuals marked a major milestone in achieving Truman's vision and reflected Johnson's keen and well-developed political skills, along with a favorable political environment. Clinton's failure to expand Johnson's achievement into universal health care reflected limited political support for comprehensive policy change, as well as shortcomings in leadership and national political expertise.

When Obama decided to run for president, he drew on all these lessons to craft a policy agenda that included affordable health care for all. By 2008, the challenges of accessing affordable health care had increased significantly, particularly for individuals with preexisting health conditions, those who needed expensive medical treatments that quickly exceeded lifetime coverage limits, and young workers whose first jobs might not include health insurance benefits. These circumstances, combined with Obama's personal health care experiences and the policy positions of his Democratic opponents in the presidential primary race, informed Obama's decision to focus on health care reform as a signature campaign issue.

CHAPTER 2

Why Did Obama Make Health Care Reform a Campaign Promise in 2008?

If there's a senior citizen somewhere who can't pay for their prescription drugs, and has to choose between medicine and the rent, that makes my life poorer, even if it's not my grandparent.... There is not a liberal America and a conservative America—there is the United States of America. There is not a Black America and a White America and Latino America and Asian America— there's the United States of America.
　　　　　　—Illinois State Senator Barack Obama, keynote address to the Democratic National Convention, 27 July 2004

Each and every time, a new generation has risen up and done what's needed to be done.... Today we are called once more, and it is time for our generation to answer that call.
　　　　　　—US Senator Barack Obama, presidential campaign announcement, 10 February 2007

We are in a defining moment in our history. Our nation is at war. The planet is in peril. The dream that so many generations fought for feels as if it's slowly slipping away. We are working harder for less. We've never paid

more for health care or for college. It's harder to save and it's harder to retire. And most of all we've lost faith that our leaders can or will do anything about it. . . . I am running in this race because of what Dr. King called "the fierce urgency of now." Because I believe that there's such a thing as being too late. And that hour is almost upon us.
—US Senator Barack Obama,
speech at Jefferson-Jackson dinner, Des Moines,
10 November 2007

If there is anyone out there who still doubts that America is a place where all things are possible, who still wonders if the dream of our founders is alive in our time, who still questions the power of our democracy, tonight is your answer. . . . And to those Americans whose support I have yet to earn, I may not have won your vote tonight, but I hear your voices. I need your help. And I will be your president, too.
—President-elect Barack Obama,
victory speech, 4 November 2008

Barack Obama's road to the White House included a vast array of personal, academic, professional, and policy experiences, many of which diverged from those of his recent predecessors. After spending his childhood in Hawaii and Indonesia, Obama completed his undergraduate education in the United States and worked in community organizing before attending law school. He entered state politics in Illinois in the mid-1990s and launched a successful US Senate campaign in 2004, gaining national attention that year with a memorable keynote address at the Democratic National Convention. Less than three years later, Obama announced his candidacy for president, which surprised some party elites and led to an intense battle for the nomination.

This chapter presents a brief summary of Obama's life and his journey to the White House, highlighting key events—both successes and failures—that broadly influenced his leadership on health care reform. Obama's rich experiences fostered a commitment to public service that, consistent with Democratic Party priorities, led to a focus on health care in the 2008 presidential campaign. Obama's early personal experiences with medical treatment issues and, as an adult, seeing his mother's stress over coverage gaps to treat her ultimately fatal illness informed his policy views when he entered politics.

Illustrating John Kingdon's classic analysis of the three main policy streams (problems, politics, and policy choices), Obama's observations of health care problems informed his commitment to health care reform in the 2008 presidential race.[1] He called for universal health care coverage shortly before he officially entered the race in 2007, recognizing the rapidly growing problems of access to health care and the cost of that care. These issues were particularly significant for Democrats, who sought to rectify the failure to enact health care reform during the Clinton presidency. Obama's victory solidified the expansion of Americans' access to health care as his administration's top priority, even as other issues such as the economy, immigration, and foreign policy demanded White House leadership as well.

Early Influences on Obama's Political Views

Barack Obama's formative years were steeped in cultural, family, and geographic diversity. Born in Hawaii on 4 August 1961, Barack Hussein Obama II was the son of two college students: freshman Stanley Ann Dunham and Barack Hussein Obama, a student from Kenya. Their marriage, which was opposed by both families, soon resulted in separation, followed by divorce. Ann Dunham was awarded sole custody of her son, and she and her parents, who were originally from Kansas, raised him primarily in Hawaii. Obama's father graduated from the University of Hawaii in three years and then pursued graduate studies in economics at Harvard University. He returned to Hawaii just once to visit when his son was in elementary school.[2]

Ann completed her undergraduate degree in anthropology and then moved with her six-year-old son to Jakarta, Indonesia, to join her second husband, Lolo Soetoro, whom she had met at the University of Hawaii. Obama lived in Indonesia until he was ten, attending Indonesian-language schools and taking English correspondence courses at his mother's insistence. In a memoir about his childhood and young adult years, Obama wrote that his mother would wake him at 4:00 a.m. five days a week to give him English lessons for three hours before school. He complained repeatedly at the time but later recognized that his mother wanted to ensure he had opportunities beyond those available in Indonesia: "She now had learned ... the chasm that separated the life chances of an American from those of an Indonesian. She knew which side of the divide she wanted her child to be on. I was an American, she decided, and my true life lay elsewhere."[3]

In fifth grade, Obama returned to Hawaii to live with his grandparents, Stanley and Madelyn Dunham. He was awarded a scholarship to attend the elite private Punahou School, where he completed his secondary education. Obama's father came for a monthlong visit the first Christmas Barack was back in Hawaii, and the senior Obama was invited to the school to speak about Kenya and his Luo ethnic group. Obama never saw his father again, although they corresponded, and Obama visited his paternal family in Kenya as a young adult. His mother returned with her toddler daughter, Maya, to pursue graduate studies in anthropology at the University of Hawaii, but when she went back to Indonesia two years later for fieldwork, Obama decided to stay with his grandparents.[4]

Obama's peripatetic childhood indirectly influenced his views on politics and policy in important ways. In Indonesia, he experienced substandard health care when his mother took him to a hospital for treatment of a deep cut, only to find two young doctors playing a game of dominos that they casually finished before stitching the wound, which left a large scar. For his mother, Obama later wrote, the turbulent political situation created "the pervading sense that her child's life might slip away when she wasn't looking, that everyone else around her would be too busy trying to survive to notice."[5] At Punahou, Obama was one of just a few African American students, and he sometimes faced curiosity and questions about his racial and family background. Though many of Obama's peers came from affluent families, his had limited financial resources, and he worked at an ice cream store to contribute to the household.[6]

Moving to the continental United States for college laid the foundation for Obama's political career. He attended Occidental College in Los

Angeles on a full scholarship and played on the junior varsity basketball team, which had an undefeated season. But Obama found the small liberal arts college, which had fewer than two thousand students when he attended, too small. After two years he transferred to Columbia University in New York City, where he completed his undergraduate degree in 1983.[7] Not surprisingly, given his future ambitions, Obama majored in political science, writing a senior thesis about nuclear disarmament in the Soviet Union. In 2007, during Obama's presidential campaign, the *New York Times* interviewed one of his former professors and a classmate, both of whom recalled that he was a good student. But, as the *Times* noted, "Barack Obama does not say much about his years in New York City."[8] Obama did not release his academic transcript from Columbia or provide the names of students, coworkers, or friends who could share their recollections of him.

Obama's later work in public service was more significant for his career than his college experience was. After graduating from Columbia, he worked briefly for a New York consulting firm that assisted multinational corporations with research on and analysis of overseas markets. He then joined the nonprofit New York Public Interest Research Group, where he encouraged students at the City College of New York to advocate for environmental policy reform.[9] In 1985 Obama moved to Chicago to work as a grassroots organizer, and he spent the next three years advocating for community development on issues such as water contamination, job training, and housing. Working in low-income neighborhoods on the South Side of Chicago introduced Obama to challenges in communities with which he had never engaged on a sustained basis. As one biographer wrote, Obama's experiences in Chicago provided "his first deep immersion into the African American community he had longed to both understand and belong to."[10]

During the 2008 presidential campaign, the *New York Times* noted that Obama devoted nearly one-third of his more than four hundred-page memoir *Dreams from My Father* to his community work in Chicago. On the campaign trail, he described that work as "the best education I ever had, better than anything I got at Harvard Law School."[11] However, after working in Chicago for a few years, Obama decided that law school was a necessary step in his professional journey. He later wrote,

"I had things to learn in law school, things that would help me bring about real change.... I would learn power's currency in all its intricacy and detail, knowledge that would have compromised me before coming to Chicago but that I could now bring back to where it was needed."[12] Despite Obama's subsequent views on the value of his legal education, going to Harvard proved to be a transformative decision both professionally and personally.

From Law School to Politics

Obama excelled at Harvard Law School, graduating magna cum laude in 1991. He received national attention in 1990 when he was elected president of the *Harvard Law Review*, becoming the first Black student in the journal's 104-year history to hold this position. In addition to his academic achievements, Obama worked as a research assistant for Laurence H. Tribe, the Carl M. Loeb University Professor and professor of constitutional law at Harvard. Tribe later described Obama as "brilliant, personable, and obviously unique."[13] Speaking to a reporter for the student newspaper, the *Harvard Crimson*, just after Obama launched his presidential campaign in 2007, Tribe characterized him as "a serious intellectual as well as a fantastic campaigner who can reach across boundaries.... He will make an extraordinarily fine president."[14] Kirkland and Ellis Professor of Law David B. Wilkins remembered Obama as "brilliant, charismatic, and focused."[15] Interviewed by the *New York Times* after his historic election to the *Harvard Law Review*, Obama reflected on its significance: "The fact that I've been elected shows a lot of progress.... But it's important that stories like mine aren't used to say that everything is O.K. for blacks."[16]

Most significant during Obama's law school years was his summer 1989 internship at a Chicago law firm, where he met his future wife and life partner. Michelle Robinson had graduated from Harvard Law School in 1988 and was working at the corporate law firm Sidley & Austin in her hometown. She served as Obama's adviser during his summer position there. Two years later, they were engaged, and Obama moved back to Chicago to work in politics.[17] By this time, he had some local name recognition. Valerie Jarrett, who hired Michelle to work in Mayor

Daley's office, became a close friend of both Obamas and served as a senior White House adviser during Obama's two terms as president. She recalled meeting him for the first time: "I didn't know him personally, but there weren't many black lawyers in the country who hadn't heard of the first black president of the *Harvard Law Review* in its then 104-year history. He also had received some local attention as a successful community organizer on Chicago's South Side before he went to law school. Plus his name is not one you forget." Jarrett thought from the start that Obama might have a future in politics, at least locally, but at the time, the White House was not even a consideration. As she wrote in her memoir, "Not in my wildest dreams did I imagine that. But I do remember thinking it was entirely plausible that he might one day even be mayor of Chicago."[18]

Obama's early post–law school years in Chicago were busy with work, writing, and family. His historic editorship of the *Harvard Law Review* led to a book contract, which resulted in the publication of Obama's 1995 memoir. He wrote the book while teaching courses on constitutional law, voting rights, and racism and law at the University of Chicago Law School.[19] He also worked for Project Vote in Chicago, organizing highly successful voter registration drives in African American neighborhoods that resulted in more than 150,000 new African American voters in the November 1992 elections.[20]

Obama's marriage to Michelle in 1992 brought lasting joy, followed by the devastating loss of his mother three years later. Ann Dunham had completed her doctoral degree in anthropology and was working on development projects in Indonesia when abdominal pains caused her to return to Hawaii, where she was diagnosed with uterine and ovarian cancer. Less than a year later, in November 1995, Dunham died at age fifty-two. She had been engaged in a stressful battle with her insurance company over its denial of disability payments, which would have covered some of her lost wages. Obama later publicly discussed his mother's health insurance issues, claiming that she had been denied coverage for a preexisting condition. In fact, her medical treatment was covered, but she had significant unreimbursed expenses.[21]

Obama worked in private practice for a few years before entering electoral politics. He joined the civil rights firm of Miner, Barnhill & Galland and continued to teach at the University of Chicago Law School. When state senator Alice Palmer, who represented Obama's district, announced her candidacy for a special election to fill an open congressional seat in 1995, Obama decided to launch his first political campaign and announced his candidacy for Palmer's state senate seat, initially with her support. But when Palmer fared poorly in the congressional primary election, she decided to run for reelection to the state senate instead. Obama stayed in the race and prevailed in the primary by successfully challenging the signatures on voter petitions submitted by Palmer and two other Democratic challengers, making them ineligible to appear on the ballot. As a result, Obama was unopposed for the Democratic nomination in a heavily Democratic district and easily won in the general election.[22]

In eight years as a state senator, Obama focused on achieving practical political goals and developing bipartisan connections. When he took office, Republicans controlled the Illinois Senate, outnumbering Democrats thirty-seven to thirty-two. To build political coalitions, Obama cultivated relations with members of both parties, negotiating patiently on policy differences and informally building networks by playing poker and golf with his colleagues. As a result, he successfully advocated for legislation on campaign finance reform, law enforcement accountability for interrogation practices and the end of racial profiling, tax credits for low-income workers, increased funding for child care, and other programs.[23] But Obama had larger political aspirations, and this soon became evident to his peers. As one Republican legislator later said, Obama "has always had his eyes on the prize, and it wasn't Springfield. If he deserves to be president, it is not because he was a great legislator."[24] National politics was the next step.

From State to National Politics

Obama's initial foray into national politics was unsuccessful, raising questions about his long-term political viability. The weekly travel required as a state senator put a strain on Obama's family life, making him reluctant to take on a bigger political commitment that would entail even more time away from home. But Obama's keen interest in a political future gained momentum with two unexpected opportunities that arose in 2004: running for a US Senate seat from Illinois and delivering a major speech at the Democratic National Convention. Success in both efforts propelled Obama into the national spotlight again, leading to a discussion of presidential possibilities. Following through on that possibility happened much more quickly than even Obama's strongest supporters anticipated.

After just a few years in the Illinois Senate, Obama set his sights on national office, deciding in 1999 to challenge Congressman Bobby Rush in the March 2000 Democratic primary. It was a risky plan, as several of Obama's friends warned him: Rush would be running for a fifth term in a district on the South Side of Chicago with a predominantly Black, Democratic, and working-class constituency. A founding member of Illinois's Black Panther Party in 1968, Rush had grown up in Chicago and had deep ties to the community, having served as an alderman before winning election to Congress. But Obama saw an electoral opportunity after Rush lost a mayoral campaign against incumbent Richard M. Daley in February 1999, even though Rush's name recognition and political support remained high. Rush interrupted his campaign in October following a devastating tragedy, when his twenty-nine-year-old son was fatally shot after leaving a grocery store. Soon after, the Illinois governor called the state legislature into special session over the winter holidays to pass gun safety legislation that had previously been overturned in the courts. Obama was in Hawaii for an annual family vacation at the time, and because his young daughter had become seriously ill, he did not return to Illinois for the special session, in which legislation failed by five votes. Obama faced harsh media and political criticism for his absence, and he lost the primary by more than 30 percent of the vote.[25]

Obama's loss raised questions from supporters about his political future and questions from his family about the feasibility of balancing politics with raising young children. The birth of his first child, Malia, in 1998 made his weekly travel to Springfield especially burdensome for his wife. When the legislature was in session, Obama spent almost half the week in the state capital, leaving Chicago on Monday evening and returning late Thursday. After his second child, Sasha, was born in 2001, Obama's commute became even more difficult for the family.

As Michelle Obama wrote in her memoir, "Five years into his tenure as state senator Barack's overloaded schedule was starting to really grate on me."[26] She was also highly skeptical about embarking on a political life, especially after the fierce criticism her husband received for missing the crime bill vote because Malia was ill in Hawaii. In the congressional campaign, Rush had described Obama as an elitist outsider, which his wife found both disappointing and offensive: "I was astonished to see how our leaders treated him only as a threat to their power," she wrote.[27]

Obama's loss to Rush hindered his national political profile and made the financial costs of a political career (while he was still paying off student loans) painfully clear. When he attended the Democratic National Convention in Los Angeles in the summer of 2000, his credit card was denied for an airport car rental, he received a limited pass for convention events, and he was denied admission to special convention parties because no one recognized him. Obama later told political strategist David Axelrod (who was a top political adviser for Obama's two presidential campaigns and worked in the White House for two years), "I felt as if I was a third wheel in this whole thing. . . . I ended up leaving early, and that was the stage when I was really questioning whether I should be in politics."[28]

Still, Obama's strong fund-raising in the congressional race, growing name recognition and expanding political network in Chicago, and new appreciation of the importance of building a solid political constituency provided valuable lessons for his political future.[29] When US Senator Peter Fitzgerald (R-IL) announced he would not seek reelection in 2004, Obama decided to enter the race.[30] Initially one of several Democratic candidates, Obama was determined to dominate the campaign. He met with wealthy donors to build a large war chest for the campaign, ultimately raising $15 million. As the *New York Times* wrote during Obama's first presidential campaign, "Even as he cultivated an image as an unconventional candidate devoted to the people, not the establishment, he systematically built a sophisticated, and in many ways quite conventional, money machine."[31]

Obama's run for the Senate unexpectedly became less competitive when a major Democratic opponent dropped out of the primary race after a former spouse made allegations of abuse. Soon after, a significant Republican contender also dropped out when allegations of sexual abuse by a former spouse were revealed in custody documents.[32] And even before the general election, Obama gained enduring national visibility with a momentous speech at the 2004 Democratic National Convention, where his reception was the polar opposite of his experience in Los Angeles just four years earlier.

Without a doubt, Obama's journey to the White House started with his 2004 keynote address at the Democratic National Convention. The campaign team of presumptive nominee Senator John Kerry (D-MA) invited Obama to deliver the speech based on recommendations from party members, as well as Kerry's own favorable impressions of Obama. The two met for the first time at a fund-raising event shortly after the Illinois Democratic primary, and Kerry took note of Obama's political skills. According to Chicago journalist David Mendell, who covered Obama's Senate campaign and attended the fund-raiser, "It's Kerry kind of looking at him and picking up tricks from the rookie. . . . That was the event where he really impressed Kerry."[33] In early July the Kerry campaign selected Obama to deliver the speech.

Obama drafted the speech himself and practiced it several times to ensure that he was ready to address the large convention audience. His extensive preparation paid off: when he delivered his seventeen-minute speech at Boston's Fleet Center on 27 July 2004, the enthusiastic audience interrupted him thirty-three times with applause.[34] Obama's confident message that the United States could move past its party and policy divisions to make unified decisions in the country's best interest was electrifying. Sharing his family's personal journey and his parents' commitment to education, Obama declared, "My story is part of the larger American story." He linked his personal successes to the promise of American politics, saying, "[we] can pursue our individual dreams and still come together as one American family." And in addressing the country's economic challenges and the ongoing wars in Afghanistan and Iraq, Obama asked people to embrace opportunities for change. He asked, "Do we participate in a politics of cynicism, or do we participate in a politics of hope?"[35] Although that hope did not result in the election of a Democrat to the White House in 2004, it certainly helped Obama's Senate race and his political future.

Without a strong Republican challenger, Obama easily prevailed in November, winning 70 percent of the vote and becoming the third African American US senator since the post–Civil War Reconstruction era.[36] In his victory speech, Obama presented a centrist political message, declaring, "We don't expect government to solve all our problems," but noting that government needed to help people obtain the necessary resources to pursue the American Dream.[37] This statement represented Obama's continuing efforts to bridge liberal and conservative views about the government's role in American politics, just as he had in his convention address.

As a senator, Obama worked diligently to complement his high public visibility and popularity with detailed attention to the inner workings of the Senate, mindful of his seniority ranking of 99th out of 100. He decided not to appear on Sunday talk shows during his first year in the Senate, and he played a key role in the passage of ethics reform legislation in 2007 that restricted gifts members of Congress could accept from lobbyists and required greater disclosure of campaign donations from lobbyists.[38] Still, Obama was a national celebrity who was regularly queried about the possibility of mounting a presidential campaign, and the appeal of doing so soon overshadowed daily legislative tasks. Two years into his Senate term, Obama announced his candidacy for president.

Decision 1: Make a Firm Commitment to Health Care Reform in the 2008 Presidential Campaign

When Obama launched his presidential campaign in early 2007, his prospects for winning the Democratic nomination, let alone the general election, seemed highly unlikely. In contrast to US senator (D-NY) and former First Lady Hillary Rodham Clinton, who had also entered the race, Obama was a relative newcomer to national politics, and some thought he was establishing the foundation for a future campaign. But Obama and his campaign team had studied the nomination contests closely and identified a path to victory that they resolutely followed from early 2007 to the caucuses and primaries in 2008. Senior Democrats, such as Senate majority leader Harry Reid, spoke privately with Obama about running for president, even as they publicly remained neutral during the nominating contests.³⁹ Through careful strategy, an inspirational campaign, and relentless competition, Obama prevailed over Clinton for the party nomination.

Even before formally starting his presidential campaign, Obama staked out a firm position on health care reform at a special conference in January 2007. Seeking to make a bold policy statement at a program sponsored by the progressive policy organization Families USA, Obama declared his commitment to enacting universal health care coverage for all Americans in his first term as president.⁴⁰ Speaking in Springfield, Illinois, a few weeks later to announce his candidacy for the Democratic presidential nomination, Obama declared, "Let's be the generation that says right here, right now, that we will have universal health care in America by the end of the next president's first term."⁴¹ This position addressed growing concerns about declining employer-based health insurance and increasing costs for individual insurance plans.⁴² At the start of the twenty-first century, nearly two-thirds of Americans (some 65 percent) had employment-based health insurance, but by 2009, that number had declined to approximately 56 percent.⁴³ The challenge of finding affordable health insurance raised significant concerns among voters about both economic stability and access to health care.

Two months later, however, at a March 2007 forum in Las Vegas, Obama faltered on health care, providing few specifics and no plan to back his pledge. In contrast to Clinton, who demonstrated a deep knowledge of health policy based on her long-standing engagement with the issue, Obama seemed unprepared for the discussion and, consequently, for the presidential race. When an audience member pointed out that Obama's campaign website contained few specifics on his health care vision, he replied, "Keep in mind that our campaign now is I think a little over eight weeks old," and he said a detailed plan would be available within the next two months. An Associated Press article about the forum asked, "Is Obama All Style and Little Substance?"⁴⁴ Determined to do better, the Obama campaign set out to conduct extensive research on health care policy and prepare a detailed policy proposal for discussion on the campaign trail.⁴⁵

Obama's commitment to health care reform reflected a growing political consensus about its importance. By the summer of 2007, Democratic and Republican presidential candidates had declared that the US health care system required significant changes. Their common focus indicated dual challenges: (1) the growing problem of access to health care, with close to forty-five million Americans lacking health insurance, compared to thirty-seven million in the early 1990s, and (2) the cost of health insurance for employers and individuals.[46] The candidates broadly agreed on reform plans, though there were significant differences between the two parties. Republican candidates, including former New York City mayor Rudolph W. Giuliani, Senator John McCain of Arizona, and former Massachusetts governor Mitt Romney, called for market-based approaches to make health insurance more available and affordable. As governor, Romney had instituted major health care reform in Massachusetts with bipartisan support, including an individual mandate for health insurance, but he said a national program would have different requirements. In contrast, Democratic candidates, including Clinton, Obama, and former US senator from North Carolina John Edwards, endorsed key components of the Massachusetts program for national reform, including a health insurance mandate for individuals and employers, as well as subsidies to purchase insurance.[47]

Winning the Democratic Nomination

Health care continued to be a major issue in the early 2008 presidential campaign, but the main focus in the race for the Democratic nomination was the Clinton-Obama competition. Understanding how Obama secured the nomination is an important factor in explaining his leadership in pursuing health care reform as president. For much of 2007, Obama lagged far behind Clinton in national polls as well as in expectations. This was due partly to Obama's inexperience in national politics but also to strenuous efforts by Clinton supporters to minimize opposition to her candidacy.

The Clinton team's strategy to winnow the field of possible Democratic presidential contenders started well before any of them, including Clinton, declared their candidacy. In March 2006 the *New York Times Magazine* reported on Democrats' hesitancy to do anything that might hinder a Clinton campaign: "So formidable are the obstacles to challenging Clinton that even a lot of party operatives who don't think she's the best candidate are likely to work for her, just to be on the winning side. And this is precisely the strategy that her team has thus far cultivated."[48] (The article focused on former Virginia governor Mark Warner as a potential Democratic presidential candidate and mentioned a few other possibilities, but not Obama.) To counter this strategy, the Obama campaign defined 2008 as a "change election"—not just a change from the policies of George W. Bush but a change from politics as usual in Washington, which was a criticism directed at Clinton.[49]

Obama highlighted this message in an inspirational speech at the Jefferson-Jackson dinner in Iowa in November 2007, which put the Clinton campaign on notice that Obama was a serious challenger for the nomination. Six Democratic presidential contenders, including Clinton and Obama, spoke to approximately nine thousand attendees about their campaign goals just a few weeks before the Iowa caucuses.[50] Obama spoke last, which was no easy task, as the event lasted more than four hours. But he mobilized the audience with a powerful call for change. His concluding remarks echoed his call at the 2004 Democratic National Convention for a new approach to policymaking that was grounded in hope, inspiration, and transformational governance: "That's why I'm asking you to stand with me, that's why I'm asking you to caucus for me, that's why I am asking you to stop settling for what the cynics say we have to accept. In this election—in this moment—let us reach for what we know is possible. A nation healed. A world repaired. An America that believes again."[51] Reporting on the dinner and the candidates' efforts in Iowa, *Time* magazine concluded, "As Clinton trudged through a week of momentum-sapping process stories . . . Obama appeared to gain energy. . . . His speech at the dinner was the performance of a politician, not a rock star. But he has found his voice."[52]

Less than two months later, Obama's momentum led to a decisive victory in the Iowa caucuses. Democratic turnout surged, nearly doubling from 125,000 in 2002 to more than 239,000 in 2008, with high participation among first-time caucus attendees, independent voters, and young voters.[53] Obama won nearly 38 percent of the vote. Clinton received 29.5 percent, narrowly losing second place to Edwards, who received closer to 30 percent. In the next two weeks, Clinton was victorious in

New Hampshire and Nevada; however, due to the proportional allocation of national delegates based on votes received across the state, Obama actually won more delegates in Nevada. Obama then won a significant victory in South Carolina, with more than double the number of votes Clinton received.[54]

Obama received a major boost following the South Carolina primary with an endorsement from Senator Edward Kennedy (D-MA).[55] Kennedy praised Obama as a candidate "who appeals to the hopes of those who still believe in the American dream ... who can lift our spirits and make us believe again."[56] Senator Kennedy's endorsement evoked the inspirational presidential leadership of his brother John, as did the endorsement of President Kennedy's daughter, Caroline. Writing in the *New York Times*, Caroline Kennedy declared, "I have never had a president who inspired me the way people tell me that my father inspired them. But for the first time, I believe I have found the man who could be that president."[57] The Kennedy endorsements were a momentous achievement for Obama and an immense disappointment for Clinton, as they signaled that major members of this Democratic political dynasty believed she could lose to Obama.[58] The Obama campaign quickly reinforced that view. Following Obama's numerous victories in the more than two dozen "Super Tuesday" nominating contests in February, Obama campaign manager David Plouffe announced, "We believe it's next to impossible for Senator Clinton to close that pledged delegate count."[59]

Clinton refused to accept defeat, battling relentlessly for the nomination through the spring of 2008. After losing several contests in February, Clinton prevailed in a number of key states, including Ohio, Pennsylvania, and Indiana. Still, Obama maintained a narrow but steady lead in pledged convention delegates, causing Clinton to ask "superdelegates"—unpledged party leaders and elected officials—to vote for her. In a letter she sent to almost eight hundred superdelegates in late May, Clinton wrote, "When the primaries are finished, I expect to lead in the primary vote and in delegates earned through primaries. . . . I hope you will consider not just the strength of the coalition backing me, but also that more people will have cast their votes for me."[60] But this effort was unsuccessful. After the nominating contests concluded in early June,

Obama was clearly ahead in delegates. Pressured by party leaders to concede, Clinton acknowledged Obama's victory and endorsed him for the Democratic nomination.[61]

Winning the Election

Despite the bitter nominating battle and some lingering tension with both Hillary and Bill Clinton, Obama succeeded in unifying the party by the time the Democratic National Convention was held in August 2008. His message for change in Washington resonated with voters as the 2008 financial crisis unfolded, and Obama presented a compelling case for his candidacy in the presidential debates. His historic victory on 4 November 2008 represented a generational change in American politics and was celebrated worldwide. Throughout the campaign, Obama maintained his firm commitment to health care reform, and after his election, he moved quickly in the transition period to establish an institutional structure in the White House for developing a legislative plan.

After prevailing in the nominating contests, Obama's major task in the summer of 2008 was ensuring Hillary Clinton's support. Some of Clinton's supporters pressed for her selection as Obama's running mate, and even Bill Clinton suggested the possibility late in the primary race.[62] But the Obama campaign did not seriously explore that option, and Obama selected Senator Joe Biden (D-DE) as his vice-presidential candidate in August, just before the party convention in Denver. Nevertheless, Clinton expressed her unqualified support for Obama on the second night of the convention, declaring in the first few minutes of her speech that "Barack Obama is my candidate. And he must be our President." Highlighting her signature policy issue, she stated that she could not wait "to watch Barack Obama sign a health care plan into law that covers every single American."[63] Obama reiterated the point in his nomination acceptance speech, announcing, "Now is the time to finally keep the promise of affordable, accessible health care for every single American."[64]

From the convention to the general election, Obama stayed on message, reiterating his campaign themes of changing politics and policymaking in Washington by energizing public opinion and building momentum for action that crossed traditional party divisions. Obama was well placed to challenge White House leadership over the past eight years and make a case for change. The ongoing wars in Afghanistan and Iraq, as well as the domestic housing and financial crises in 2008, had sharply decreased President Bush's approval ratings and hindered Republican John McCain's campaign. As Obama said in the third presidential debate at Hofstra University in October 2008:

> The policies of the last eight years and—and Washington's unwillingness to tackle the tough problems for decades has left us in the worst economic crisis since the Great Depression. And that's why the biggest risk we could take right now is to adopt the same failed policies and the same failed politics that we've seen over the last eight years and somehow expect a different result. We need fundamental change in this country, and that's what I'd like to bring.[65]

On election night, Obama's victory was evident soon after the polls closed. He won several key states, including Democratic strongholds such as Pennsylvania, and states that had voted Republican in the 2004 presidential election, including Iowa, New Mexico, and Ohio.[66] High Democratic turnout and the support of independents, young voters between the ages of eighteen and twenty-nine, and Black voters were crucial to Obama's victory.[67] Democrats also increased their majorities in Congress, picking up twenty-one seats in the House and eight seats in the Senate (which became a filibuster-proof majority of sixty seats in the summer of 2009).[68] Speaking in Chicago after McCain conceded the election, Obama did not directly reference the historic significance of his election as the first African American president of the United States. But with his first words about the power of democracy to achieve the American Dream, his message was clear. Stressing unity over party, Obama declared, "Americans have never been a collection of red states and blue states; we are, and always will be, the United States of America."[69]

In the following weeks, Obama put that optimistic message into practice. He moved swiftly to identify his White House team and nominees for positions in the cabinet and the Executive Office of the President that required Senate confirmation. The day after the election, he announced his transition team, which was headed by seasoned Washington political advisers John Podesta (chief of staff in the Clinton presidency), Pete Rouse (Obama's Senate chief of staff), and close friend Valerie Jarrett.[70] In keeping with his promise of unity, Obama nominated Hillary Clinton for secretary of state and asked Secretary of Defense Robert Gates to continue in that position.[71] Obama's nomination of Senator Tom Daschle (D-SD) for secretary of health and human services led to unexpected controversy. Daschle had lost his reelection campaign (and his position as Senate majority leader), and after reports of unpaid taxes surfaced, Daschle withdrew his nomination. Obama then nominated Kansas governor Kathleen Sebelius, who was confirmed.[72] To help navigate his promised health care plan through Congress, Obama appointed an expert legislative affairs team headed by longtime Capitol Hill senior staffer Phil Schiliro.[73]

Conclusion

From his globe-trotting childhood to his ascent to the White House, Obama developed qualities of adaptability, interpersonal engagement, initiative, and leadership. These personality traits, combined with his academic success, public visibility, and historic presidential election victory, raised high expectations for achievement in the White House. The economy was clearly voters' major concern in 2008. Exit polls found that 63 percent of respondents identified the economy as the most pressing national issue, while only 9 percent cited health care as the top priority.[74] Still, following through on his campaign pledge, Obama made health care his signature issue in his first year in office. The path from promise to reality would require the president's firm and continuing attentiveness, as well as resilience and political versatility to address unexpected obstacles to policy reform.

CHAPTER 3

Obama's Early Presidential Leadership and Policymaking Efforts

Nearly a century after Teddy Roosevelt first called for reform, the cost of our health care has weighed down our economy and the conscience of our nation long enough. So let there be no doubt: health care reform cannot wait, it must not wait, and it will not wait another year.
—Barack Obama, address to a joint session of Congress, 24 February 2009

Well, the time for bickering is over. The time for games has passed. Now is the season for action. Now is when we must bring the best ideas of both parties together, and show the American people that we can still do what we were sent here to do. Now is the time to deliver on health care.
—Barack Obama, remarks to a joint session of Congress, 9 September 2009

With today's vote, we are now incredibly close to making health insurance reform a reality in this country. Our challenge then is to finish the job.... For the sake of our citizens, our economy, and our future, let's make 2010 the year we finally reform health care in the United States of America.
—Barack Obama, remarks on Senate passage of health care reform legislation, 24 December 2009

Upon taking office in January 2009, Obama confronted the worst US financial crisis since the Great Depression. In the first few months of his presidency, he oversaw passage of an economic stimulus package and a bailout of the automobile industry through loan guarantees to help the nation regain its financial footing. With such pressing priorities, health care reform risked being postponed until the economic situation stabilized. But Obama was determined to press forward, and he had a more favorable policy environment for doing so than Clinton, the last Democratic president to attempt a comprehensive overhaul of health care, did in 1993.

Addressing health care reform was a complex task. Democrats generally concurred on the need for expanded access to health insurance and greater affordability, and interest groups were willing to support reform because it would benefit their constituencies.[1] But these broad areas of agreement encompassed many difficult questions about how to make health care accessible and affordable, leading to significant intraparty and interparty debates. Navigating these debates to build majority support for legislation required dedicated, persistent, and sustained presidential leadership.

Through the spring and summer of 2009 the White House and Congress worked on health care reform. Legislators took the lead in developing reform bills, and the president's top health care and legislative advisers communicated regularly with key House and Senate committees. Amid growing criticism from opponents of health care reform, President Obama participated in town hall meetings around the country to address public concerns about his proposals. To demonstrate his commitment to moving forward with health care reform, Obama addressed Congress on the topic in September. By the end of the year, the House and Senate had each passed a bill to make health care more affordable and available to Americans, albeit with significant differences that would have to be dealt with in conference discussions.

Decision 2: Identify Health Care Reform as an Immediate Priority in 2009

After passing economic rescue legislation during his first month in office, Obama turned to health care. Several close advisers recommended that he concentrate on some other priority, such as climate change or immigration, instead of taking on the contentious and complicated issue of health care reform, but Obama was determined to follow through on his campaign promise to make health care more accessible and affordable.[2] Following his first message to Congress in late February, Obama convened a special White House forum with legislators, doctors, union leaders, and representatives of businesses, hospitals, and insurers to discuss some of the key challenges to health care reform, including cost, types of coverage and plans, and requirements for participation.[3] Overcoming congressional disagreements about these topics was the White House's primary task in 2009, with the goal of developing legislation that Congress could pass and that met the administration's objectives.

Deciding to proceed with health care reform was no easy decision for the Obama administration, given the complexity of the US medical system and the politically charged debates over how to make health care more accessible and affordable. Despite his limited Washington experience, Obama had surprised many by prevailing in the hotly contested nomination battle in 2008, and he had promised to move beyond partisan disputes in policymaking. Concentrating on some other issue, such as economic recovery, likely would have gained broader political support for the new president. As two scholars of American politics noted, by focusing on health care reform, "President Obama was putting the prestige of his popular presidency on the line."[4] The president did so in his first address to Congress on 24 February 2009, stating that health care reform could not "wait another year." Although Obama's speech was largely about the state of the economy and his recovery plan, he devoted a full section to health care, which he identified as the United States' second investment priority, in between energy and education. Citing "the crushing cost of health care," Obama promised "a historic commitment to comprehensive health care reform—a down-payment on the principle that we must have quality, affordable health care for every American."[5]

Decision 3: Exercise White House Leadership to Start the Policymaking Process for Health Care Reform in the Spring of 2009

Two weeks later, the Obama White House hosted a forum on health care reform attended by approximately 150 people representing the many components of the health care industry. The event linked long-term economic recovery, including deficit reduction, to less burdensome medical care for Americans, particularly the forty-six million who lacked health insurance.[6] Following opening remarks by the president, the group divided into five breakout sessions with insurance executives, labor leaders, policy analysts, lobbyists, and Democratic and Republican lawmakers. Afterward, Nancy-Ann DeParle, director of the White House Office of Health Reform, observed that several participants who had previously opposed reform efforts, including someone connected with the organization responsible for the "Harry and Louise" ads critical of President Clinton's health care proposal, indicated a willingness to support bipartisan legislation.[7]

Obama's call for health care reform in his first address to Congress, followed by his White House forum on the topic, illustrated the president's commitment to enacting legislation expeditiously. But Obama was also determined to avoid the mistakes of the Clinton administration, particularly the failure to consult Congress from the outset. Consequently, the Obama White House largely deferred to congressional leaders to draft legislation, but with significant input from the administration throughout the process.[8] In addition, they recognized the importance of having the House and Senate develop their own proposals independently before creating a single unified bill.[9]

Congress had an instructive bipartisan model for drafting health care legislation: the successful enactment of market-based health care reform in Massachusetts. Republican governor and future presidential candidate Mitt Romney had worked with a predominantly Democratic state legislature to pass the Massachusetts law, which required almost all employers to provide health insurance for their workers and created a state-subsidized plan with access to medical and dental care for people who lacked health insurance.[10] In the 2008 presidential race,

Democratic candidates endorsed several key aspects of health reform in Massachusetts, including an individual mandate to have health insurance, an employer mandate to provide health insurance, and subsidies to help people purchase insurance. More extensive reform proposals, such as eliminating private insurance and establishing universal health care coverage through a public program—popularly described as "Medicare for all" or a single-payer system—were viewed as transformative but politically impractical.[11] Obama stated during the campaign, "If I were designing a system from scratch, I would probably go ahead with a single-payer system."[12] But given the major institutional changes required to create such a system, Obama endorsed more incremental reforms, although he did call for a government-run health care plan that would compete with private insurance.

Democratic reluctance to endorse more progressive reform proposals reflected an economic approach to policymaking that prioritized efficiency over the expansion of rights such as health care equality.[13] This view had guided Democratic policymaking since the late twentieth century and informed the Obama administration's broad guidelines to Congress in 2009 with regard to which health care policy goals to incorporate into legislation.[14] But navigating the wide range of Democratic views on health care reform—from progressive calls for a public health insurance option or a single-payer system to more conservative efforts to employ market-based approaches to make health insurance more cost-efficient—would be challenging.[15]

In the Senate, several Democratic leaders guided the legislative debate in multiple committees. Senator Ted Kennedy (D-MA), a staunch advocate of guaranteed access to health care for all Americans, had endorsed his state's law and pursued a comparable plan in the spring of 2009 as chair of the Senate Health, Education, Labor, and Pensions (HELP) Committee. Tragically, Kennedy's tireless efforts ended with his untimely death from brain cancer in the summer of 2009. In addition to Kennedy, Senate Finance Committee chair Max Baucus of Montana had been working with the committee's ranking Republican, Chuck Grassley of Iowa, since the summer of 2008 on developing a health care plan.[16]

Shortly after the 2008 election, Baucus released a nearly hundred-page paper presenting a vision for health care reform. Although the paper explicitly stated that it was not a "legislative proposal," it addressed the key topics that would be covered by such legislation: "health care coverage, quality, and cost."[17] This document became the foundation for legislative planning by Baucus and Grassley, who had played a key role in drafting a Republican counterproposal to President Clinton's health care plan in the 1990s.[18] They convened a working group consisting of themselves, two Senate Democrats—Jeff Bingaman of New Mexico and Kent Conrad of North Dakota—and two Senate Republicans—Mike Enzi of Wyoming and Olympia Snowe of Maine. Members of this group, which became known as the Gang of Six, represented multiple ideological positions in each party, ensuring that competing concerns and interests would be considered.[19]

Bringing Democrats and Republicans together to craft health care legislation explicitly addressed the missed opportunity to do so in the 1990s. The Republicans' alternative to Clinton's proposal had not been presented in time to take legislative action before campaigning for the 1994 midterm elections overtook the policy agenda. After Democrats lost control of both chambers of Congress in 1994, partisan conflict heightened significantly. Efforts to build bipartisan coalitions were overshadowed by minority-party strategies to block legislation and represent party interests.[20] As a result, by 2009, bipartisan negotiations were not feasible in the House, given the stark differences between Democrats and Republicans over the need for health care reform.

In the Senate, bipartisan discussions led by Baucus and Grassley presented a glimmer of hope for legislation. By building on the Republican plan from the 1990s, which included an individual mandate for health care coverage and access to insurance options through health care exchanges, Baucus tried to develop a proposal that would gain solid support in both parties.[21] But over the past decade, partisan conflict and governance had increased in the Senate as well.[22] Despite early promising efforts, differences along party lines with regard to minimum plan requirements and cost soon became clear. Furthermore, intraparty disagreement arose among the Democrats, as did conflicts between the White House and Congress. As Obama later wrote: "The more everyone dug into the details of reform, the more differences in substance and strategy emerged—not just between Democrats and Republicans but between House and Senate Democrats, between us and congressional Democrats, and even between members of my own team."[23] These disputes accelerated in the summer of 2009, raising serious questions about the possibility of bipartisan legislation and about Obama's ability to fulfill his campaign promise to enact health care reform.

Decision 4: Defer to Congress to Develop Health Care Legislation in the Summer of 2009

As negotiations over health care reform continued on Capitol Hill in the spring and summer of 2009, the White House engaged in the policymaking process but deferred to congressional leadership to determine what was politically feasible. In the House, Democrats sparred over the extent of health care coverage and the scope of reform. In the Senate, the handful of Democrats and Republicans charged with pursuing bipartisan efforts considered multiple legislative possibilities but ultimately could not agree on a plan of action. Seeking to build public support, Obama participated in town hall meetings to address people's concerns, but these sessions sparked significant opposition from critics. By the end of the summer, the prospects for moving forward with legislation were uncertain at best.

Obama had built an expert team to advance his policy agenda. Secretary of the Department of Health and Human Services (HHS) Kathleen Sebelius had been the governor of Kansas (leaving three years into her second term to serve in Obama's cabinet) and, before that, state insurance commissioner. Jeanne Lambrew, director of the HHS Office of Health Reform, was a health care policy expert in academe and government, having served on the faculty of the University of Texas's Lyndon B. Johnson School of Public Affairs and as a health analyst for the National Economic Council and the Office of Management and Budget (OMB) in the Clinton administration. White House Office of Health Reform director Nancy-Ann DeParle had worked in OMB and served as director of the Health Care Financing Administration, overseeing Medicare, for the Clinton administration.[24]

Additionally, several of Obama's top White House advisers were highly influential in guiding the legislation through Congress, given their longtime experience on Capitol Hill. Chief of staff Rahm Emmanuel had served in the Clinton White House, advising the president on political affairs, policy, and strategy; he later represented Illinois for six years in the House of Representatives, where he chaired the Democratic Caucus. Deputy chief of staff Jim Messina had participated in several congressional campaigns and had been Senator Baucus's chief of staff. Director of legislative affairs Philip M. Schiliro had worked on Capitol Hill for more than two decades, including as chief of staff for Congressman Henry Waxman, chair of the House Oversight and Government Reform Committee, and as policy director for Senator Tom Daschle during Daschle's tenure as minority leader.[25] Obama could count on these officials, as well as Vice President Joe Biden, to take advantage of their lengthy and distinguished careers on Capitol Hill to advocate for the president's priorities and assess congressional reactions. Obama's top White House advisers on health care reform, such as DeParle, met regularly with members of Congress to hear their views on policy prospects and possibilities, working largely behind the scenes to avoid the perception that Obama's team was directing legislative proposals.[26]

To build a political coalition in Congress, the White House had to maintain a delicate balance between advocating for administration priorities and allowing the policymaking process to engage legislators' various interests and concerns. Addressing the American Medical Association (AMA) in June, Obama declared, "If we do not fix our health care system . . . America may go the way of G.M." (referring to the recent bankruptcy of General Motors).[27] Fixing the health care system, though, required deferring to the legislative process. Liz Fowler, who served as chief health policy counsel to Baucus during the drafting of the Affordable Care Act and later worked for the Obama White House, noted on the act's ten-year anniversary that a key component of Obama's leadership "was really giving Congress enough space to be able to write legislation."[28] A retrospective analysis of the ACA's passage similarly identified how the president "outlined his general principles" and then deferred to congressional committees "to formulate their own bills."[29] Building on his longtime experience on Capitol Hill, Schiliro recognized the importance of avoiding legislative stalemate by "let[ting] the two branches pass their own bills and negotiate the differences."[30]

At the same time, the White House provided both formal and informal guidance as both chambers of Congress developed their initial legislative proposals. Obama declared that economic recovery was directly linked to health care reform, and the February 2009 stimulus package included funding to computerize health records and conduct research on the merits of medical procedures.[31] The March 2009 White House forum included participants from the medical, hospital, pharmaceutical, and insurance industries, including many people who had previously opposed health care reform.[32] As *Washington Post* reporter Ceci Connolly said, "Every single one of those people gathered at the March White House summit wanted one thing: a seat at the table."[33] Their engagement was encouraging, but it also led to certain expectations, such as not creating a public option or government-run health plan to compete with private health insurance.[34]

Obama recognized the political constraints early in the process, demonstrating his awareness of the need for pragmatism over transformation. In his June speech to the AMA, Obama outlined a few key goals: electronic records, preventive care, a medical cost structure that was not dependent on tests and services for compensation, lower expenses for medical education, and increased availability of medical information for practitioners, among others. Obama acknowledged, however, that these goals did not require a public option for health insurance. As he stated, "What we seek is more stability and a health-care system on a sound financial footing. And these reforms need to take place regardless of what happens with a public option."[35] In any case, opposition from the health care industry and limited political will in Congress would likely block any proposal for a single-payer health insurance system or one in which the federal government oversaw health care for the entire population, similar to the system in Canada. Seeking to address concerns about the possible loss of existing health care options, Obama famously promised (twice), "If you like your doctor, you will be able to keep your doctor. Period. If you like your health care plan, you will be able to keep your health care plan. Period."[36] This turned out to be incorrect, as discussed in chapter 5 on implementation of the ACA.

With potential White House constraints in the background, summer negotiations in the House of Representatives focused on the challenge of expanding access to health care while managing costs. In mid-July the House Ways and Means Committee passed legislation to expand access to health insurance through federal subsidies, require employer funding for workers' health care, and create a government-run health program to give individuals another option alongside private plans.[37] The AMA endorsed the legislation—H.R. 3200: America's Affordable Health Choices Act of 2009—and pledged in a letter to committee chair Charles B. Rangel (D-NY) to help "expand access to high quality, affordable health care for all Americans."[38] Despite support from the primary group representing physicians, which had historically opposed government involvement in health care, strong disagreements were evident. The committee approved the bill by a vote of twenty-three to eighteen, with three Democrats joining Republicans to vote against the bill. Of particular concern was a warning by the Congressional Budget Office (CBO) that the legislation would not halt the rapid increase in medical costs and would actually contribute to those costs. As CBO director Doug Elmendorf told the Senate Budget Committee, "The legislation significantly expands the federal responsibility for health care costs."[39]

By the end of July, two more House committees had passed health care legislation. Just hours after the Ways and Means Committee's vote, the House Education and Labor Committee passed almost the same bill by a vote of twenty-six to twenty-two, with four Democratic and all Republican committee members opposed. Among their concerns were proposed tax increases, including a payroll tax for employers that did not provide health insurance for their workers, to offset the cost of health care for uninsured individuals.[40] Two weeks later, the House Energy and Commerce Committee passed its version of the Affordable Health Choices Act by a vote of thirty-one to twenty-eight, with five Democrats and all Republicans voting against the legislation. Committee chair Henry Waxman (D-CA) successfully mediated disagreements between conservative and liberal Democrats, achieving some cost savings by having public health plans work with pharmaceutical companies to set drug prices and using those savings to lower health insurance premiums for many Americans. But the bill did not include a single-payer health care system operated by the government, much to the disappointment of liberal Democrats. And of course, progress in the House did not mean support in the Senate.[41]

Initial negotiations in the Senate were more focused on bipartisan possibilities due to the efforts of the Gang of Six. Following Obama's White House summit in March, Baucus and Grassley hosted three roundtables with medical industry and health policy professionals to discuss the possibility of legislative reform.[42] These roundtables raised some concerns, as Senator Baucus had received more than $2.5 million in the past few years from interest groups in the health industry, and five of his former staffers, including two chiefs of staff, now worked for experts in the field. Protesters interrupted the second roundtable in May, angry that Baucus had not allowed advocates for a single-payer health care system to testify, and he had the protesters removed and arrested.[43]

Concerns about special interests guiding legislative priorities increased in June, when the White House announced an agreement with the pharmaceutical industry to provide discounts on prescription drugs through Medicare. Baucus played a major role in developing the agreement with the Pharmaceutical Research and Manufacturers of America (PhRMA), a drug industry trade organization headed by former congressman Billy Tauzin. Although the agreement would be highly beneficial for senior citizens, it would not provide funding to support expanded access to health care.[44] Liberals and conservatives alike criticized the plan: liberals said negotiators should have secured more assistance for health care reform from pharmaceutical companies, and conservatives said the pharmaceutical industry should not have negotiated with the White House on health care, given concerns about both the overall cost of expanded access and greater federal involvement.[45]

In mid-July the Senate HELP Committee passed a bill very similar to the one approved by the House Ways and Means Committee. Despite efforts to achieve bipartisan consensus, the Senate bill was approved along party lines, thirteen to ten.[46] Furthermore, six senators—both Democrats and Republicans, including two from the Finance Committee—asked the Senate leadership to slow down the process to ensure that all concerns were addressed. Three of the senators conveyed the same message to President Obama.[47] Baucus continued to insist that the

Finance Committee could develop a bill that responded to both parties' concerns, but the differences between them proved too deep to reconcile. Still, Baucus pressed forward, even though the White House recommended that his committee pass a bill with just Democratic votes. As Obama later reflected, "Unlike the other committee chairs, who'd passed their bills on straight party-line votes without regard for the Republicans, Baucus continued to hope that he could produce a bipartisan bill. But as summer wore on, that optimism began to look delusional."[48]

To build public support for health care legislation and thereby put pressure on members of Congress, Obama hosted several town hall meetings in August in states where people had expressed significant concerns about reform, including Arizona, Colorado, Montana, and New Hampshire. Describing the meetings afterward, Obama noted that participants were highly engaged and came up with thoughtful questions and comments, whether or not they supported the administration's reform proposals.[49] In addition to the concerns expressed in the meetings, protesters gathered outside and angrily denounced both the plans and Obama. Many of these protesters represented the new Tea Party movement that had started earlier in the year and was composed primarily of conservative Republicans who opposed the stimulus package and the auto industry bailout.[50]

Members of Congress who held their own town hall meetings on health care were also greeted by disruptive hecklers, leading to the cancellation of some of these events. Some protesters angrily criticized the government's role in health care in general, castigating even Republican officials hosting the meetings as they voiced their objections to the Obama administration's agenda.[51] Other protesters had specific concerns, such as fear that the administration would permit health care decisions by "death panels"—a phrase coined by 2008 Republican vice-presidential candidate Sarah Palin in a Facebook post that was quickly shared on social media and quoted by commentators.[52] Obama and Democratic members of Congress repeatedly had to rebut ominous warnings about the consequences of health care reform, including an alarming comment by Senator Grassley to Iowa constituents: "We should not have a government program that determines you're gonna pull the plug on Grandma."[53]

By late August, Obama's approval ratings had dropped nearly twenty points since he took office, and the battles over health care reform were the main reason.[54] Senator Kennedy's absence, after he lost a yearlong battle with brain cancer, was deeply felt in Congress, where his legislative leadership and stalwart commitment to universal health care had been, in his words, "the cause of my life."[55] Kennedy had briefly attended the White House forum on health care and addressed the group immediately after the president, an indication of his political seniority and stature. Afterward he advised Obama, "This is the time, Mr. President. Don't let it slip away."[56] With critics now dominating the public debate, Obama was acutely aware that, absent a major turn of events, the opportunity to achieve health care reform might be lost.

Decision 5: Refocus Legislative Efforts on Health Care Reform in the Fall of 2009

To reset the health care debate after a tumultuous summer of unexpected and angry protests, Obama decided to deliver a special address to Congress in September. His two immediate predecessors had done the same for major policy issues: George W. Bush announced the war on terror one week after the 9/11 terrorist attacks, and Bill Clinton devoted an entire speech to health care reform in September 1993, just as Obama was planning to do sixteen years later.[57] Obama noted in his White House memoir, "Despite the inauspicious precedent, we decided it was worth a shot."[58] Memorable, even historic, speeches had propelled Obama's political career and brought him to the White House, and this presidential address aimed to build on that record.

Obama started his hourlong address to Congress on the evening of 9 September 2009 with the good news that policy decisions of the past year had "pulled this economy back from the brink." But, Obama said, "we did not come here just to clean up crises. We came to build a future." Health care, he said, was essential to that future: "I am not the first President to take up this cause, but I am determined to be the last."[59] He quoted from a letter Senator Kennedy had written in May, with the request that it be delivered after his death. Kennedy described health care reform as "the great unfinished business of our society" and "a moral issue." "At stake," he wrote, "are not just the details of policy, but fundamental principles of social justice and the character of our country."[60]

As Kennedy had envisioned, Obama outlined a legislative plan with three key components: (1) requiring the following guarantees from insurance companies—coverage of preexisting conditions, maximum limits on out-of-pocket expenses, and coverage of routine checkups and preventive care at no additional charge; (2) creating an insurance exchange where the uninsured could explore their health insurance options and companies could compete for their business, with tax credits to offset insurance premiums, if needed; and (3) requiring all individuals to have health insurance to ensure the viability of the system. Overall, the speech was well received and prompted a bump in public approval for health care reform. The news, however, was dominated by the unseemly interruption of Obama's speech by South Carolina congressman Joe Wilson, who shouted, "You lie!" when Obama said the bill would not provide health care coverage for undocumented immigrants.[61]

In calling for an insurance exchange for uninsured Americans, Obama implicitly acknowledged that a public option for health insurance might not be included in reform legislation. Republican critics of a public option insisted it would pave the way for a government-run health care program; as Senator Judd Gregg (R-NH) said, "A public plan is essentially a stalking horse for a single-payer plan."[62] But the issue was highly contentious within the Democratic Party as well. Some members strongly favored a government-run health care program, or "Medicare for all."[63] Offering a public option in a national exchange would allow people to compare the public plan with private plans and decide which one best met their needs.[64] Yet many of the so-called Blue Dog, or economically centrist, Democrats "had issues with the public option," whereas an insurance exchange of private plans would work within the existing system of health insurance.[65] Senator Kent Conrad (D-ND) declared that the exchanges would produce "much of what those who want a public option are calling for . . . something to compete with private for-profit insurance companies."[66]

Democrats also had to navigate controversial debates about which procedures health insurance policies would cover. Congressman Bart Stupak (D-MI), some other House Democrats, and House Republicans insisted that legislation include a stipulation prohibiting the use of federal subsidies to purchase an insurance plan with abortion coverage and that any government-operated plan, such as a public option, not provide such coverage. Since the mid-1970s, the Hyde Amendment (renewed annually as part of the federal budget process) had banned the use of federal Medicaid funds to pay for abortion, with exceptions for life-endangering medical conditions or pregnancy resulting from rape or incest. Stupak declared that the stipulation was consistent with the Hyde Amendment, with the same exceptions included.[67] Critics said the restriction would set a precedent for broadening the definition of subsidies to include tax breaks—such as the tax incentive for employers to provide health insurance for their employees—and then imposing requirements on health care coverage.[68] Stupak succeeded in mobilizing a coalition to add the amendment to the health care legislation, with 176 Republicans and 64 Democrats voting for the measure and 194 Democrats voting against it.[69]

With the addition of the Stupak Amendment, the House passed historic health care legislation on the night of Saturday, 7 November 2009, exactly three years after Democrats won control of both chambers of Congress in 2006. H.R. 3962—the Affordable Health Care for America Act—passed 220–215 on a predominantly party-line vote, with one Republican, Congressman Anh Cao of Louisiana, voting for the legislation and thirty-nine Democrats voting against it.[70] Consistent with Obama's September speech, the House bill extended health care coverage to some thirty-six million people who were uninsured and prohibited insurance companies from denying coverage for preexisting conditions and from dropping people who become ill.[71] It also created a health insurance exchange where people could compare plans, including a public option administered by the federal government, and make their selections.[72] Days before the vote, House Republicans introduced a bill that promised lower costs by not requiring health insurance coverage, not providing subsidies for health insurance, and not raising taxes. But without majority control, they had no chance of passing the bill.[73]

The House's passage of health care reform marked a significant achievement for the Obama administration. The president played a visible part in the final negotiations, visiting Capitol Hill hours before the vote to ensure support from Democratic lawmakers.⁷⁴ He encouraged them to make history, saying, "Opportunities like this come around maybe once in a generation. . . . Answer the call of history, and vote yes for health insurance reform for America."⁷⁵ The subsequent legislative victory provided some justification for the strategy of letting Congress take the lead in drafting a bill. Although Obama identified the overarching goals of health care reform, he largely avoided getting involved in the intricacies of House and Senate policy debates, adopting what a House Democrat described as "a laissez-faire strategy." White House chief of staff Rahm Emmanuel said the administration gave "leeway to legislators to legislate . . . [but] not leeway to take a policy off track."⁷⁶

Guiding health care reform through the Senate was a more daunting task. Despite Baucus's lengthy efforts to build bipartisan consensus, the sharp differences between Democratic and Republican policy views were evident in the summer of 2009. The Gang of Six met regularly, sometimes twice a day, to develop a plan, but their steadfast objections could not easily be reconciled. Republicans firmly opposed a government-run insurance plan as well as an income surtax for high wage earners to cover the cost of expanded access to health care. Democrats insisted that legislation make health care financially accessible to all Americans. Obama had wanted each chamber of Congress to pass a bill before the August recess, but not even the five committees developing health care legislation could meet that deadline, let alone the full House and Senate chambers.⁷⁷ As Senator Grassley, the Republican minority leader on the Finance Committee, said in late July, "There are a lot of tough decisions to make, and they aren't going to be made real quickly. . . . Most of our caucus feels that just simmering for people's reflections would be a good thing to do."⁷⁸

By the end of the summer, it was clear that there was no possibility of achieving bipartisan health care legislation in the Senate. Democratic leaders had set 15 September as the deadline for the Senate Finance Committee to pass a bipartisan bill, but the inability to do so was evident well before that date.⁷⁹ Obama hosted Baucus and Grassley in the Oval Office in early September to discuss the sources of disagreement, and Grassley raised five criticisms of the current legislation. Obama then said, "Let me ask you a question, Chuck. If Max [Baucus] took every one of your latest suggestions, could you support the bill.... Are there *any* changes—any at all—that would get us your vote?" Grassley replied, "I guess not, Mr. President."[80] That acknowledgment reflected Grassley's increasing critiques of Democratic proposals and his insistence on multiple requirements, including "no public option, no pay-or-play, no things that are going to lead to any rationing of health care, no interference with doctor-patient relationships, and tort reform."[81] To enact health care reform, Obama needed all sixty Senate Democrats to support legislation so they could end a filibuster, or at least fifty votes to pass legislation through a special process known as reconciliation (discussed in chapter 4).[82]

Uniting the Senate Democratic coalition behind health care reform required painstaking negotiations by majority leader Harry Reid of Nebraska. Reid, who had started his first term in the Senate more than two decades ago, appreciated the intricacies of providing incentives to solidify tentative Democratic votes. That was his focus, as he was convinced that winning over even a single Republican, such as Olympia Snowe of Maine, would not happen. Obama sometimes intervened in the negotiations in an effort to keep provisions that Reid thought were not politically feasible, and the senator had to remind him, "Mr. President, you know a lot more than I do about healthcare policy. But I know the Senate, okay?"[83]

Reid solidified support from Democrat Mary Landrieu of Louisiana by promising extra Medicaid money for her state, and he agreed to lower a tax on medical device manufacturers to gain the votes of a group of midwestern senators.[84] To guarantee the endorsement of Joseph I. Lieberman of Connecticut, who was officially an independent but caucused with the Democrats, Reid agreed to drop the provision creating a public option for health insurance and not to permit people between the ages of fifty-five and sixty-five to purchase insurance through Medicare.[85] Both these concessions were highly unpopular with a number of Democrats. Former Vermont governor, presidential candidate, and Democratic National Committee chair Howard Dean said dropping the public option meant the end of prospects for health care reform. Still, Obama supported Reid's decision, viewing it as necessary to move forward with legislation that year.[86]

With these compromises, the Senate moved closer to a vote on health care in December. To ensure that all sixty Democrats would support the bill, Reid reached an agreement with Ben Nelson of Nebraska that exempted his state from paying for Medicaid expansion, which meant the federal government would cover the cost instead.[87] Nelson also insisted that the legislation prohibit the use of federal funds to pay for abortion. The week before Christmas, the AMA endorsed the legislation, saying it "advances many of our priority issues for achieving a vision of a health system that works for patients and physicians."[88] On 24 December the Senate passed an $871 billion health care reform bill along party lines, with all sixty Democrats voting for the bill and thirty-nine of forty Republicans voting against it. (Republican Jim Bunning of Kentucky opposed the bill but was absent during the vote.) Afterward, Obama noted that the United States was "finally poised to deliver on the promise of real, meaningful health insurance reform.... If passed, this will be the most important piece of social legislation since the Social Security Act passed in the 1930s."[89]

Conclusion

The passage of health care bills in both chambers of Congress in 2009 marked a major victory for President Obama. The House and Senate bills contained multiple areas of agreement for expanding health care coverage, including the creation of health insurance exchanges for individuals and small businesses to find affordable coverage; subsidies to help families with limited incomes (up to 400 percent of the poverty level for a family of four, or $88,000) purchase health care coverage; the expansion of Medicaid eligibility, albeit for a larger group in the House bill; and a prohibition on the denial of coverage for preexisting conditions or based on a person's gender or medical history.

The two bills also had significant differences, including costs—$871 billion for the Senate bill and $1 trillion for the House. The House bill proposed to pay for expanded health care coverage through additional taxes on wealthy Americans (individuals earning more than $500,000 and families earning more than $1 million annually) and reductions in Medicare spending. The Senate bill reduced Medicare spending, increased Medicare taxes on families earning more than $250,000 annually, and imposed a tax on insurance companies that provided so-called Cadillac health plans that exceeded a certain cost.[90] Perhaps most important, the House bill included a public option for health insurance, which was highly popular among many of the president's supporters, while the Senate bill did not.[91] Resolving these differences would be no easy task and would require engaged, sustained leadership by President Obama in the coming months, particularly given a major unexpected change in the Democratic margin of victory in the Senate.

The partisan vote in each chamber of Congress was both unsurprising and consequential. House Republicans described the reform proposals as a "government takeover" and "a wrecking ball to the entire economy."[92] Congressman Paul Ryan from Wisconsin (Republican vice-presidential candidate in 2012 and Speaker of the House from 2015 to 2019) declared, "This is perhaps the worst bill I have seen come to the floor in my 11 years in Congress."[93] Even moderate Republican Olympia Snowe, who had been part of Senator Baucus's bipartisan group, declared that she was "extremely disappointed" with the Senate bill. Once Senate Democrats confirmed their sixty votes, she said, "Democrats had no incentive to reach across the aisle."[94] Given that party leaders in both chambers had been unable to reach agreement on priorities for health care reform, Republican critiques of the Democrats' plans were expected, and realistically, they could not be addressed without changing fundamental Democratic goals on access to health insurance and specific coverage guarantees. Nevertheless, forging ahead with legislation that lacked bipartisan support complicated both enactment and implementation of the final law.

CHAPTER 4

Obama Succeeds in Enacting the Affordable Care Act

This is a complex issue, and the longer it was debated, the more skeptical people became. I take my share of the blame for not explaining it more carefully to the American people. . . . Here's what I ask Congress, though: Don't walk away from reform. Not now. Not when we are so close. Let us find a way to come together and finish the job for the American people.
—Barack Obama, State of the Union
address, 27 January 2010

So here's the bottom line. We all know this is urgent. And unfortunately over the course of the year . . . this became a very ideological battle. It became a very partisan battle. And politics I think ended up trumping practical common sense. . . . What I'm hoping to accomplish today is for everybody to focus not just on where we differ, but focus on where we agree because there actually is some significant agreement on a host of issues.
—Barack Obama, White House Health
Summit, 25 February 2010

By necessity, leaders have to speak to [legislators'] different concerns. It isn't always tidy; it is almost never easy. But perhaps the greatest—and most difficult—challenge

> *is to cobble together out of those differences the sense of common interest and common purpose that's required to advance the dreams of all people—especially in a country as large and diverse as ours.*
> —Barack Obama, remarks at the signing of the ACA, 23 March 2010

At the start of 2010, Obama's prospects for enacting health care reform seemed promising. In November and December 2009, respectively, the House and Senate had passed separate bills that would require significant negotiations to create consensus legislation. Still, the passage of legislation in each chamber, albeit almost entirely on party-line votes, indicated the possibility of a compromise bill reaching the White House. But that possibility suffered a major setback in mid-January when Democrats lost their sixty-vote majority in the Senate due to a surprise Republican victory in the special election to fill the seat held by the late Senator Ted Kennedy. Losing the ability to end a filibuster meant the Democrats faced a high bar to enact health care legislation, particularly because no Republican senators (and only one House Republican) had voted for the initial bill.

To address the seemingly insurmountable opposition, the Obama White House focused almost exclusively on health care for the next few weeks, hosting public events and working closely with Democratic leaders in Congress to pursue a legislative strategy that would require a simple majority rather than a filibuster-proof supermajority to pass a bill. Through determined presidential leadership and skillful coalition building by the Democrats in Congress, Obama succeeded in signing historic health care legislation in March 2010.

Losing a Filibuster-Proof Majority

Senator Kennedy's death in the summer of 2009 left a progressive leadership chasm in Congress, particularly in the area of health care. Kennedy had long advocated for health care reform, and he had encouraged Obama to commit to the issue in the 2008 presidential campaign. Despite the loss of Kennedy's policy knowledge and legislative expertise, Democrats anticipated no difficulty holding Kennedy's seat in solidly liberal Massachusetts. The party's shocking loss in the January 2010 special election, however, created an unexpected obstacle to health care reform by leaving the Democrats one vote short of a filibuster-proof Senate majority. Consequently, the White House needed to reshape its legislative strategy if it hoped to fulfill Kennedy's vision of "health care in America as a right and not a privilege."[1]

In large part because of the health care debate, in late September Massachusetts governor Deval Patrick selected former Kennedy aide Paul G. Kirk Jr. to serve as senator until a special election could be held in January. Although, under Massachusetts law, the seat was supposed to remain vacant until the special election, the state legislature approved the naming of an interim senator, as Kennedy had requested before his death.[2] Kennedy's wife and two sons endorsed Kirk, who said he would not run in the special election. Kirk had worked for Kennedy in the 1970s and chaired the Democratic National Committee; at the time of his appointment to the Senate, he was chairman of the John F. Kennedy Library. During his short time in office, the seventy-one-year-old Kirk was expected to endorse the party's and the late senator's policy agenda.[3] In fact, Kirk's backing was essential for passage of the Senate's health care bill in December, as all sixty Democratic supporters were needed to overcome a filibuster in multiple procedural motions before the official vote.[4]

In early September Massachusetts attorney general Martha Coakley became the first Democrat to announce her candidacy for Kennedy's Senate seat. She quickly became the front-runner in the race, winning the support of a large political network, particularly the women's groups that had been key to Hillary Clinton's 2008 victory in the Massachusetts presidential primary.[5] Coakley's position strengthened when former congressman Joseph P. Kennedy II announced that he would not run for his uncle's seat, thereby confirming that a Kennedy would not be a candidate. (Senator Kennedy's widow, Vicki, had already said she would not seek the office.)[6] In the December primary, Coakley easily prevailed over three other Democratic contenders, winning close to 50 percent of the vote and beating the second-place candidate by almost twenty percentage points. News reports announced Coakley's likely victory in the special election, pointing out that Massachusetts had not elected a Republican senator in nearly forty years. As one commentator noted, "The election is over. . . . We have to vote in January, but the outcome is preordained. Coakley will win."[7]

Defying all predictions, the victor in the special election was Massachusetts state senator Scott Brown. Brown had overwhelmingly won the Republican primary in December, garnering nearly 90 percent of the vote, but he had to contend with limited name recognition and low expectations. As he admitted in his primary victory speech, "You may not have heard of me before now."[8] A fellow Massachusetts Republican described Brown's uphill battle against Coakley, saying, "It's tough to win against somebody with name recognition in the state."[9] Still, Brown campaigned vigorously, whereas Coakley was less assertive in making her case to voters. When a reporter for the *Boston Globe* asked whether she should engage more with voters, Coakley responded, "Standing outside Fenway Park? In the cold? Shaking hands?"[10] This perceived dismissiveness, combined with Coakley's mistake on talk radio when she called former Red Sox pitcher Curt Schilling a Yankees fan, may have cost her the election. On 19 January 2010 she lost the race, 52 to 47 percent, and conceded shortly after the polls closed.[11]

Brown's surprise victory prompted swift reactions from leaders in both political parties. Republicans declared that Massachusetts voters, whose turnout was the highest for a nonpresidential election in thirty years, had rejected Obama's legislative agenda. The stinging rebuff of Coakley represented the state's first election of a Republican US senator since 1972 and the state's first Senate victory by a Republican for a seat held by a Democrat since 1946.[12] Senator John Cornyn of Texas declared that "Democrats nationwide should be on notice: Americans are ready to hold the party in power accountable for their irresponsible spending and out-of-touch agenda, and they're ready for real change in Washington."[13] Democrats, including White House senior adviser David Axelrod, credited Brown's connection with voters and identified major flaws in Coakley's efforts. When the Coakley campaign criticized national Democrats for not actively supporting her until the week before the election, the party harshly rebutted the critique. One Democratic official said her advisers "failed to keep Coakley on the campaign trail, failed to create a negative narrative about Brown, failed to stay on the air in December while he was running a brilliant campaign."[14]

Like the Coakley campaign, the Obama White House was slow to recognize the intense voter dissatisfaction in Massachusetts. A week before the special election, White House press secretary Robert Gibbs said Obama was not planning to campaign for Coakley, even though some polls showed a tightening race and indicated that a plurality of likely voters opposed Obama's health care plan.[15] As Coakley continued to lose support in preelection polls, including among voters who viewed Obama favorably, the president participated in a Boston rally with her the weekend before the election. He urged his supporters to vote for Coakley, saying this race would decide "whether we're going forward, or going backwards" and noting, "if you were fired up in the last election, I need you more fired up in this election."[16] Two days later, Gibbs reported that Obama was "both surprised and frustrated" by Coakley's loss, particularly in a historically Democratic state where, just two years earlier, Obama had won more than 60 percent of the vote.[17]

After the special election, Obama compared Brown's victory to his own win in 2008, observing that anger and frustration produced highly motivated voters. In a television interview he stated, "The same thing that swept Scott Brown into office swept me into office. . . . People are angry and they are frustrated. Not just because of what's happened in the last one or two years, but what's happened over the last eight years." The president also warned that Democrats should not rush to pass legislation before Brown took office; instead, they should work with Republicans to find "core elements" of agreement.[18]

Critics within the Democratic Party said the Massachusetts special election illustrated shortcomings in the White House's legislative strategy. Summarizing those views, one analysis found that "the administration and national party leaders failed to show up in competitive states . . . and adequately explain to voters the nuts and bolts of initiatives like health care." Democrats were disappointed in Obama "for failing to convert his historic White House win and personal popularity into a coherent national vision that would keep the public on his side."[19] On Capitol Hill, one Democratic staffer described the mood as "a shock that will affirm the conventional wisdom that the Democratic majority in the

House is in mortal danger, that Obama can be stopped, that his entire legislative program will be halted. . . . Fear was palpable in the corridors on the Hill."[20] Obama faced the substantial challenge of demonstrating that he could keep his campaign promise and follow through on his first-year efforts to deliver health care reform without a Democratic supermajority in the Senate.

Decision 6: Continue to Advance Health Care Reform after the Democrats Lose Their Filibuster-Proof Senate Majority in January 2010

Following the Massachusetts special election, Obama focused on reorienting his legislative strategy to enact health care reform. Within the White House, the president and his domestic policy team assessed how to unify Democrats and possibly bring some Republican legislators on board. Externally, Obama's public appeals were designed to exert political pressure on Congress to take action. In late February the White House hosted a major bipartisan summit with members of Congress in an attempt to bridge policy differences. Together, these efforts kept health care central on the legislative agenda and produced momentum for both the House and Senate to move forward.

Assessing the 2010 political environment a decade later in his memoir, Obama questioned whether the standard explanations for the loss of the Massachusetts Senate seat were correct. He acknowledged that fewer policy priorities on his legislative agenda, greater attention to the Coakley campaign, and his increased presence in Massachusetts in the weeks before the special election could have made a difference. At the same time, Obama reflected that circumstances did not favor a better outcome for Democrats. Although individual weaknesses affected the loss in Massachusetts, Obama noted, "It's equally possible . . . that given the grim state of the economy, there was nothing we could have done—that the wheels of history would have remained impervious to our puny interventions."[21]

Nevertheless, Obama and his White House advisory team needed to forge a new path forward for health care reform. Chief of staff Rahm Emmanuel had been criticized by progressive Democrats for concessions he made to the health care industry during the 2009 negotiations, and he offered to step down after the loss of Kennedy's seat, but the president would not accept his resignation. Despite Emmanuel's conflicts on Capitol Hill and sometimes even within the White House on the scope of health care reform, the passage of bills in the House and Senate was due in no small part to his intensive negotiations. As Axelrod noted in early 2010, health care "would be dead a thousand times before but for Rahm's leadership."[22]

Despite the daunting road ahead, Obama and Phil Schiliro, the president's director of legislative affairs, envisioned the possibility of passing legislation on a party-line vote. If the House passed the Senate bill, the legislation could go directly to the president through a special process known as budget reconciliation.[23] But this strategy would require intensive White House leadership in Congress, close collaboration with party leaders, and a number of intermediate victories to achieve the ultimate policy goal. Back in September 2009, Schiliro had asked Obama whether he felt lucky about the prospects for health care reform. Obama had pointed out that his full name was Barack Hussein Obama and they were sitting in the Oval Office together, so, "Brother, I *always* feel lucky." In January 2010 Schiliro asked Obama, "You still feeling lucky?"[24]

Before pursuing this new legislative strategy, Obama publicly affirmed his commitment to building a bipartisan coalition for health care reform. Delivering his State of the Union message on 27 January 2010, Obama declared that Americans had faced trying times throughout history when prospects for progress seemed bleak, from the Civil War to World War II to the civil rights movement. He explained: "These were the times that tested the courage of our convictions, and the strength of our union. And despite all our divisions and disagreements, our hesitations and our fears, America prevailed because we chose to move forward as one nation, as one people. Again, we are tested. And again, we must answer history's call." To advance health care reform, Obama asked members of Congress to review his plan again and added, "If anyone from either party has a better approach that will bring down premiums, bring down the deficit, cover the uninsured, strengthen Medicare for seniors, and stop insurance company abuses, let me know. . . . I'm eager to see it."[25] Opponents were skeptical, though, and Virginia governor Bob McDonnell declared in the official Republican response that "most Americans do not want to turn over the best medical care system in the world to the federal government. Republicans in Congress have offered legislation to reform health care, without shifting Medicaid costs to the states, without cutting Medicare, and without raising your taxes." Furthermore, he said, "our solutions aren't 1,000-page bills that no one has fully read, after being crafted behind closed doors with special interests."[26] The fault lines between the two parties on health care were clear.

Two days after his speech, Obama participated in a ninety-minute session with House Republicans during their annual retreat in Baltimore to discuss policy priorities, including health care. The televised event started with a standing ovation for the president and focused on civil, substantive discussion, despite the clear political differences between Obama and his audience. House Republican leader John Boehner said in his introduction that Washington officials "need to listen to each other," and Obama stated, "We have got to close the gap a little between the rhetoric and the reality."[27] But opportunities for agreement were lacking, as vividly demonstrated by the contentious exchanges between the president and Congressmen Jeb Hensarling of Texas and Paul Ryan of Wisconsin about the cost of the White House's health care plan.[28] Obama said that even though Republicans' attacks on him and his policy agenda sharply restricted opportunities for bipartisanship, he still enjoyed the meeting, declaring, "I'm having fun. . . . This is great."[29] Nevertheless, there seemed to be no bipartisan path forward.

In addition to criticism from Republicans, Obama faced dissension within his own party. He met with Senate Democrats in early February in a televised session at the Newseum, a museum in Washington, DC, where he assured lawmakers, "I'm there in the arena with you." But when the on-record session ended and the president departed, senators expressed their disappointment with White House leadership to Obama's advisers. Senator Bill Nelson of Florida told Axelrod, "The president needs to be more hands-on with the health-care bill," while Senator Carl Levin of Michigan asked, "What exactly is the plan? What is the strategy?" Axelrod listened to the critiques and defended the president, asserting, "This thing would have been dead 15 times before now if he hadn't been persistent and committed. I don't know anybody in my memory who has expended more of his own political capital on an issue than he has on this one."[30]

Buoyed by his energetic meeting with House Republicans, Obama announced in an interview during the Super Bowl pregame show in early February that he would host a half-day bipartisan summit on health care later in the month. As he explained, "I want to come back and have a large meeting, Republicans and Democrats, to go through systematically all the best ideas that are out there and move it forward."[31] In addition to its substantive purpose, the timing of the summit gave House Democratic leaders an opportunity to build support for the Senate bill, which was less far-reaching than the House bill in terms of coverage options. Obama insisted that the legislative process build on the 2009 bills, while Republicans recommended a new start if the president wanted their support. As Senate minority leader Mitch McConnell (R-KY) said, "If we are to reach a bipartisan consensus, the White House can start by shelving the current health spending bill."[32]

Ultimately, the seven-hour televised summit at Blair House (the president's guesthouse, located across the street from the White House) illustrated the sharp and seemingly irreconcilable partisan differences over health care reform. Republicans reiterated that the president should scrap the existing House and Senate bills and start anew, but Obama refused to consider that possibility, pointing out that Americans wanted action now. If Republicans refused to work with Democrats, he said, then the White House and the Democratic leadership in Congress would forge ahead, try to pass legislation independently, and see how the voters responded. As Obama famously declared, "That's what elections are for."[33] His 2008 promise to change Washington policymaking faded as the window to pass health care reform became increasingly narrow.

In pursuing health care reform in early 2010, Obama continued to publicly tout the importance of bipartisanship. Yet, as indicated by his speeches and remarks at legislative meetings, he was skeptical about finding common ground. As a result, Obama's legislative team began to pursue an alternative plan to use the special budgetary procedure of reconciliation to enact legislation with a simple majority vote. But to do so, the president had to accomplish the daunting task of winning his party's support for the Senate bill in the House.

Sacrificing the House Bill for the Senate Bill

Obama's success in passing the ACA was dependent on the resolute leadership of House Speaker Nancy Pelosi. Despite her own reservations about the Senate bill, Pelosi understood that, after the Massachusetts special election, there was no path forward for the House bill. Consequently, Pelosi was faced with the delicate and arduous task of unifying House Democrats in support of legislation that would do less than they had hoped to accomplish. This would ensure that Obama could follow through on his signature campaign promise, albeit less extensively than the president and his supporters had originally envisioned.

Pelosi's two decades in Congress and her family's deep engagement in politics and public service prepared her well for the difficult task she faced in early 2010. The child of Baltimore mayor Thomas D'Alesandro Jr., Nancy attended her first political convention at age twelve and attended President John F. Kennedy's inaugural ball when she was twenty. She graduated from Trinity College in Washington, DC, where she met Paul Pelosi, a student at Georgetown University. They moved to his hometown of San Francisco a few years after marrying. The Pelosis had five children in six years, and while the children were still young, Nancy started to work for the California Democratic Party, recruiting candidates and raising funds.[34]

At age forty-seven, when her youngest child started college, Pelosi ran for Congress and won a special election in 1987 to serve in the House of Representatives. She rose in the House to become party whip, minority leader, and then Speaker after the Democrats won control of both chambers of Congress in 2006. The first woman to serve in this position and the second in line for the presidency, after the vice president, Pelosi was acutely aware of how her prepolitical career had prepared her for legislative leadership. She said, "Nothing prepared me for being Speaker of the House more than the values, discipline, interpersonal skills, the logistics, the quartermastering—all that you have to do to raise a family while never taking your eye off the children."[35]

Pelosi worked assiduously in 2009 to build a legislative coalition in support of health care reform. Initially, she had been skeptical about the possibility of securing Republican votes, asking Emmanuel, "Does the president not understand the way this game works? He wants to get it done and be beloved, and you can't have both—which does he want?"[36] After securing passage of a House bill in November through multiple intraparty compromises, Pelosi was unwilling to negotiate further. However, the House and Senate bills still had important differences, particularly the higher cost of the House plan. In January 2010 Obama worked closely with House and Senate Democrats to negotiate a compromise, but when the Senate team presented concessions, Pelosi said, "The House will give you nothing."[37] Nevertheless, the White House appeared to be close to reaching an agreement until Brown's win in the Massachusetts special election derailed the possibility of a filibuster-proof path to victory.

Pelosi pivoted quickly to ensure that health care reform would still move forward. Although the Senate bill appeared significantly flawed compared to the House bill, the new political reality meant that the Senate's plan would have to be the basis of reform. Of her approximately 250-member Democratic caucus, Pelosi needed 216 votes to pass the Senate bill (slightly less than the typical 218 out of 435 votes needed for a majority, due to vacancies). Pelosi estimated that she could count on some 180 votes at the outset, which meant she and the White House had to persuade about 40 Democrats to advance the legislation. Pelosi was confident of success and told reporters: "You go through the gate. If the gate's closed, you go over the fence. If the fence is too high, we'll pole vault in. If that doesn't work, we'll parachute in. But we're going to get health care reform passed for the American people."[38]

Decision 7: Enact the ACA through the Budgetary Process of Reconciliation in March 2010

To move forward with health care reform, the White House now had to pursue a complicated legislative strategy. If the House passed the Senate bill, the two chambers could then pass, by a simple majority vote, another bill that made small changes to the first through a budgetary process known as reconciliation. This process was created by the Congressional Budget Act of 1974 to expedite the passage of tax, spending, and debt limit legislation. Under reconciliation, bills cannot be filibustered in the Senate, and amendments are restricted as well. Congress may consider up to two reconciliation bills in a calendar year, typically a budget resolution for each fiscal year (which begins on 1 October). In the decades following passage of the 1974 law, the reconciliation process was used for deficit reduction legislation, welfare reform in 1996, and tax cuts in 2001 and 2003.[39]

Even before the special election in Massachusetts, the Obama White House had considered the possibility of using reconciliation to enact the Senate's health care bill and then make small modifications with a simple majority vote. As the Coakley-Brown race tightened in January 2010, news reports discussed the reconciliation option as well as the possibility of rushing a bill through Congress while Democrats still had sixty votes in the Senate, but the latter option did not have the support of the White House or legislative leaders. One report noted that "the time window for such a move would be tight, and the move might be politically unpalatable."[40] As noted earlier, Obama was firmly opposed to any effort to pass the bill before Senator-elect Brown was seated, stating: "I just want to make sure that this is off the table: The Senate certainly shouldn't try to jam anything through. . . . People in Massachusetts spoke. [Brown's] got to be part of that process." Senate majority leader Harry Reid (D-NV) concurred, telling reporters, "We're not going to rush into anything. . . . We're going to wait until the new senator arrives before we do anything more on health care."[41]

Passing the Senate bill in the House would be no easy task, particularly given the tortuous path the House had taken to pass its own more generous health care legislation the previous November. Still, Pelosi firmly agreed that the House needed to pass the Senate bill, telling Obama, "Well, that's not even a question, Mr. President. . . . If we let this go, it would be rewarding . . . the Republicans for acting so terribly, wouldn't it? We're not going to give them the satisfaction."[42] Although Pelosi had previously secured a Democratic majority in the House, several members now expressed concerns about the cost of health care reform, particularly those whose reelection prospects in 2010 were uncertain.

At an estimated cost of $871 billion, the Senate bill was nearly $200 billion less than the House bill, but the amount was still a significant concern for some Democrats. Dennis Cardoza (D-CA), who voted for the House bill but expressed reservations about spending, said, "I think we can do better." Frank Kratovil Jr. (D-MD), who voted against the House bill, noted, "The system is broken; we have to do something. . . . But my preference would be to do smaller things." Some House Democrats pointed out that the Senate bill contained less restrictive language on abortion coverage than the House bill, and others criticized the lack of a public health insurance option in the Senate bill.[43]

Traditionally, House-Senate disagreements are addressed in conference committee sessions. These discussions result in a revised bill that must be approved by both chambers before it is sent to the president for signature. But without the possibility of conference committee negotiations, the White House had to secure a House Democratic coalition to pass the existing Senate bill, with minimal changes, through reconciliation.

The dogged efforts of Obama, Pelosi, and their legislative leadership teams succeeded in building a narrow House coalition to enact the Senate bill. To get there, a wide range of concerns had to be addressed, particularly about abortion and Medicare funding. Socially conservative Democrats questioned the Senate bill's language prohibiting the use of federal funds to pay for abortion by means of health insurance premium subsidies and insurance exchanges, favoring the stricter language of the House bill's Stupak Amendment. Other concerns among House Democrats included geographic differences in Medicare payments for states and the lack of a public option for health insurance in the Senate bill. Pelosi insisted that there would be no separate votes on abortion, a public option, or other contentious topics, as doing so could derail the bill's passage via reconciliation. Still, Pelosi worked assiduously behind the scenes to bring wavering Democrats on board, and she assuaged some members' concerns about the use of taxpayer funds to pay for abortions. (The only Republican who voted for the House bill in November 2009 voted against the ACA in March 2010 because Democrats had not done enough to restrict abortions.)[44] Democrats successfully addressed the issue of state disparities in Medicare funding and gained some support by reinstituting federal aid for state hospitals involved in charity care.[45]

In the event Democrats lacked sufficient votes to pass the bill, party leaders considered using a complicated legislative procedure that would allow the House to pass the Senate bill without an actual vote on the legislation. With this procedure, known as "deem and pass," the bill could become law without requiring Democrats who objected to certain provisions to cast a vote either for or against it.[46] Republicans expressed strong objections to the strategy, which they declared was likely unconstitutional. *Wall Street Journal* columnist Peggy Noonan criticized the plan as "Demon Pass."[47] Ultimately, Democrats decided to move ahead with a House vote, anticipating that they had the numbers to secure victory.[48]

As the prospect of a House vote neared, Obama postponed a planned trip to Australia and Indonesia. He spoke with Democrats about the historic importance of enacting health care reform and addressed concerns among some party members that the White House had left too much of the legwork of developing politically viable legislation to Congress.[49] After several days of speaking one-on-one with dozens of caucus members, the president traveled to Capitol Hill the day before the vote to appeal to the full House Democratic caucus. In a half-hour speech, Obama encouraged Democrats to move forward, saying, "This is the single-most-important step we have taken on the health care system since Medicare . . . I believe good policy is good politics."[50] But outside the Capitol, protesters booed as Obama's motorcade passed by, holding signs with messages such as "Get your hands out of my pocketbook and health care."[51]

Nevertheless, Obama's call for congressional action sealed Democratic support, and the House passed the Senate bill by a vote of 219–212 on 21 March 2010. All the votes in favor of the legislation were cast by Democrats, while all 178 Republicans and 34 Democrats opposed it.[52] Of the thirty-nine Democrats who had voted against the House bill in November 2009, twenty-eight did so again, and eleven changed their votes and supported the bill in March. Six members who had voted for the November bill opposed the March legislation.[53] Before the vote, Pelosi commented on the historic importance of the legislation, saying it would "restor[e] the American dream" by "complet[ing] the great unfinished business of our society" and adding that health care "is a right and not a privilege."[54]

In explaining their decision to vote for the bill, House Democrats spoke of the need to support the president and achieve long-awaited progress on health care reform. Dan Maffei (D-NY), who voted for both bills (albeit with some concerns about the Senate bill that were ultimately addressed), said, "We've debated this bill long enough. . . . Doing nothing is no longer an option."[55] Ohio congressman Dennis Kucinich expressed concerns that the bill did not provide enough protections for individuals, but he voted for health care reform in March after voting against it in November. As he explained in a news conference, "We have to be very careful that the potential of President Obama's presidency not be destroyed by this debate. . . . There's something much bigger at stake here for America."[56]

On 23 March 2010 President Obama signed the Patient Protection and Affordable Care Act, popularly known as Obamacare, into law.[57] Speaking at the White House, Obama declared that "all of the overheated rhetoric over reform will finally confront the reality of reform. . . . The bill I'm signing will set in motion reforms that generations of Americans have fought for, and marched for, and hungered to see."[58] After introducing Obama, Vice President Joe Biden famously whispered to the president, not realizing that the media could hear him, "This is a big f****** deal!"[59] The new health care law included the following provisions:

- Individuals would be required to purchase health insurance, with subsidies and hardship exemptions available based on income, or pay a penalty.
- Companies with more than fifty employees would be required to provide health care coverage.
- Health insurance exchanges would be created to assist small businesses, self-employed individuals, and unemployed individuals in purchasing health care coverage.
- Medicaid coverage would be expanded significantly.
- Children could be covered by their parents' health care plans until age twenty-six.

- The Medicare payroll tax would increase for families making more than $250,000 annually and for insurance companies that provided expensive, popularly known as Cadillac, health care plans.

- Federal funding for abortion coverage would be banned for people purchasing health insurance through the exchanges, with exceptions for rape, incest, or danger to the mother's life.

- Undocumented immigrants would not be eligible to purchase insurance through the exchanges.[60]

One week after enacting the ACA, Obama signed reconciliation legislation, which the House had passed by a 220–211 vote and the Senate had passed by a 56–43 vote. The reconciliation package made some budgetary modifications to the ACA, including:

- Phasing out by 2020 the Medicare prescription drug coverage "donut hole," which created a gap in coverage for drugs costing within a certain range.

- Creating incentive programs to reward high-quality Medicare Advantage plans (provided by Medicare-approved private companies) with higher payments.

- Increasing funding to combat health care fraud.[61]

Reflecting on the night the House passed the health care bill, Obama noted that those celebrations were more significant to him personally than his election night victory. "This was a celebration that mattered," he wrote. "Winning the election had been extraordinary, but it had been just a promise. . . . This night meant more to me, a promise fulfilled."[62]

Conclusion

Fulfilling the promise of health care reform in 2010 required Obama to pursue a multipronged leadership strategy. First, he had to respond to critiques of the White House plan from legislators, addressing both intra- and interparty concerns. Second, he needed to work closely with his party's leadership in the House, particularly Speaker Pelosi, to solidify a coalition that would pass the Senate's 2009 plan, and then he had to confirm support in both chambers of Congress for a reconciliation bill to make minor budgetary changes. Third, Obama had to make a strong public case for health care reform to pressure Congress to take action before the midterm elections.

After successfully pursuing these strategies to enact the ACA, Obama's next task was implementing the law. This would be a daunting challenge with many formidable obstacles, as the president clearly recognized. Speaking to Nancy-Ann DeParle late on the afternoon of 21 March, after calling several House members before the vote, Obama cautioned, "This law better work. Because starting tomorrow, we own the American healthcare system."[63] Taking ownership, ensuring that Americans had access to the protections guaranteed by the ACA, and advocating for the law's constitutionality would dominate the rest of the Obama presidency.

CHAPTER 5

Obama's Health Care Reform Legacy
Implementing and Upholding the ACA

Earlier today, the Supreme Court upheld the constitutionality of the Affordable Care Act.... In doing so, they've reaffirmed a fundamental principle that here in America—in the wealthiest nation on Earth—no illness or accident should lead to any family's financial ruin.
—Barack Obama, 28 June 2012

It has now been six weeks since the Affordable Care Act's new marketplace has opened for business. I think it's fair to say that the rollout has been rough so far.... It is a complex process. There are all kinds of challenges. I'm sure there will be additional challenges that come up.... But we've got to move forward on this.
—Barack Obama, 14 November 2013

If I had told you eight years ago that America would ... secure the right to health insurance for another 20 million of our fellow citizens ... you might have said our sights were set a little too high. But that's what we did.
—Barack Obama, farewell address, 10 January 2017

After signing the ACA into law, Obama faced a complex implementation process. Some provisions of the law were instituted quickly, such as requiring insurance companies to provide access to some preventive health care services without cost. Larger components, such as the creation of a marketplace where people could compare health insurance plans before purchasing one, were scheduled to begin a few years later, given their complexity. Along the way, the ACA faced and survived challenges from multiple states that questioned its constitutionality, particularly the health insurance mandate. Despite many obstacles and complications related to implementation, the ACA's enduring features were in place when Obama's presidency ended in 2017. But affordable health care for Americans who were not eligible for ACA subsidies remained a challenge, as did managing the costs of health care.

Almost from the moment Obama signed the ACA into law, its constitutionality was challenged. Several Republican-led states filed suit over the federal government's mandate that individuals carry health insurance, claiming it violated state sovereignty. The Obama administration tried to address this issue by offering states more flexibility in how they provided health insurance, but those efforts did not assuage opposition to the law. In the first decade after the ACA's enactment, the Supreme Court ruled three times on its constitutionality, each time upholding the law's central features. Thus, the Obama administration was able to move forward with implementation, despite some rollout difficulties, and preserve the law's primary goal of expanding access to affordable health care for many Americans.

Initial Effects of the ACA

After the ACA became law in 2010, certain key provisions went into effect almost immediately. Insurance companies were prohibited from denying coverage to children due to preexisting medical conditions. Lifetime limits on insurance coverage for benefits such as hospital stays ended. Senior Americans received a onetime $250 rebate check (not subject to taxes) to compensate them for the Medicare prescription drug "donut hole," or gap in coverage. Young adults now had the option of remaining on their parents' health insurance plan until age twenty-six if they lacked their own health care coverage. States became eligible to receive additional federal matching funds for expanding health care coverage for low-income families through Medicaid.[1]

The expansion of health care services under the ACA continued in 2011. Many of these services benefited senior Americans, such as prescription drug discounts, preventive care, and post-hospital stay care.[2] In response to states' concerns, the White House announced in February that it would support accelerating the granting of innovation waivers to states that expanded access to health care. Waivers would be granted as long as states provided coverage to as many residents as would receive health care under the ACA. As the White House announced, "The proposal offers States more flexibility while ensuring that all Americans, no matter where they live have access to affordable, accessible health insurance. Additionally, the proposal includes built-in protections to ensure that these waivers do not increase the Federal budget deficit."[3]

The Obama administration's willingness to endorse flexibility in implementing the ACA reflected the political reality following the 2010 midterm elections. Democrats lost sixty-three seats in the House of Representatives, as well as party control of that chamber; they lost six seats in the Senate but retained party control there.[4] Passage of the ACA contributed to these losses, as incumbents who supported the law were viewed as more ideologically liberal than, and thereby more distant from, their constituents.[5] Following the 2010 elections, Obama acknowledged his party's difficulties with public opinion, famously admitting that he took a "shellacking" and explaining, "The responsibilities of this office are so enormous . . . [that] sometimes we lose track of the ways that we connected with folks that got us here in the first place."[6]

In particular, Obama attributed Democratic losses to the bargaining and negotiations that led to the ACA's passage, describing that process as an "ugly mess." Nevertheless, although Obama "regret[ted] that we couldn't have made the process more healthier than it ended up being," he affirmed that "the outcome was a good one."[7] Expanding on this point in his memoir, Obama reflected, "The election didn't prove that our agenda had been wrong. It just proved that—whether for lack of talent, cunning, charm, or good fortune—I'd failed to rally the nation, as FDR had once done, behind what I knew to be right. Which to me was just as damning."[8] The communication skills that propelled Obama to national attention in 2004 and defined his 2008 presidential campaign did not fundamentally shift public opinion on Obama's signature policy goal of health care reform.

The Supreme Court Upholds the Constitutionality of the ACA

Minutes after Obama signed the ACA into law in March 2010, fourteen states filed legal challenges in federal court. Florida and twelve other states charged that the law infringed on state sovereignty by exceeding Congress's power to regulate interstate commerce and violating the Tenth Amendment's protection of the states' exercise of power in areas not prohibited by the Constitution or subject to federal jurisdiction. The states' attorneys general said the ACA's penalty for noncompliance with the individual mandate amounted to an unconstitutional direct tax. Virginia filed a separate lawsuit that challenged the ACA partly on the grounds that it violated a recent state law protecting residents' right to refuse health insurance. The Florida lawsuit declared that the ACA violated the liberty of individuals to decide whether to carry health insurance. Furthermore, the ACA's expansion of Medicaid required states to defer to the federal government to direct and administer those programs.[9] When the lawsuit reached the Supreme Court in the 2011–12 term, twenty-six states were plaintiffs.[10]

After the Supreme Court heard oral arguments in the spring of 2012, President Obama publicly declared that overturning the law would exceed the court's authority, and he did not expect that to happen.[11] As Obama stated, "Ultimately, I am confident that the Supreme Court will not take what would be an unprecedented, extraordinary step of overturning a law that was passed by a strong majority of a democratically elected Congress." He said overturning the ACA would amount to judicial activism and noted, "For years, what we have heard is, the biggest problem on the bench was judicial activism, or a lack of judicial restraint, that an unelected group of people would somehow overturn a duly constituted and passed law." He added, "Well, this is a good example, and I'm pretty confident that the court will recognize that and not take that step."[12]

Obama's expectations proved correct, and in June 2012 the Supreme

Court ruled five to four to uphold the ACA. Chief Justice John Roberts and the four liberal justices (Clinton appointees Ruth Bader Ginsburg and Stephen Breyer, and Obama appointees Sonia Sotomayor and Elena Kagan) said Congress's constitutional authority to levy taxes permitted the ACA's requirement that most Americans have health insurance or pay a penalty.[13] Upholding the health insurance mandate through the taxation provision of the Constitution was a surprise, as Roberts agreed with the four conservative justices (Reagan appointees Antonin Scalia and Anthony Kennedy, George H. W. Bush appointee Clarence Thomas, and George W. Bush appointee Samuel Alito) that Congress's power to regulate interstate commerce did not provide constitutional protection for the requirement. These same five justices also ruled that the ACA could not mandate Medicaid expansion, finding that states could choose to keep their existing Medicaid programs and payments instead of broadening access to Medicaid and receiving increased federal funds to do so.

With the Supreme Court's ruling, the Obama administration could proceed as planned with implementation of the ACA. Much of the law was slated to go into effect by 2014, which gave the White House about a year after the 2012 presidential election to help states create health insurance exchanges, develop a federal health insurance exchange for states that did not have their own exchanges, and publicize the health insurance acquisition process to the public. The complexity of this process, combined with ongoing partisan opposition, created multiple complications during the rollout in the fall of 2013.

Putting the Full ACA into Practice

Despite Democratic losses in the 2010 midterm elections, Obama won reelection by a solid margin in 2012, campaigning largely on the accomplishment of enacting the ACA. But Republican opposition to the law hindered implementation in 2013, particularly in the wake of a sixteen-day federal government shutdown in October. After the government reopened, the process for accessing information on health insurance exchanges proved to be extraordinarily complicated, and people experienced numerous difficulties in signing up for health insurance.

Ultimately, the White House brought back two senior policy advisers to smooth the implementation process, which eased the transition tremendously. Although the ACA continued to face judicial and political challenges in subsequent years, the core goal of expanding Americans' access to health care remained intact and made significant progress during and after Obama's presidency.

Obama touted the ACA's benefits as a signature issue in his 2012 reelection campaign. Even though a majority of the American public still opposed the law, the White House steadfastly supported its provisions and even embraced the term "Obamacare," which critics had used pejoratively. As campaign spokesperson Stephanie Cutter explained, "Republicans spent hundreds of millions branding Obamacare as a negative, and we believe we can turn that to our advantage."[14] Public opinion surveys showed that many voters viewed health care as a decisive issue in 2012, with only the economy and jobs outranking it in importance.[15] With Republican presidential candidate Mitt Romney calling for the law's repeal, voters had a clear choice between the two major-party candidates on this issue. A 2012 study noted that "each candidate offer[ed] fundamentally different visions for the nation's health care system."[16] Combined with the Supreme Court's ruling upholding the law, Obama's reelection ensured that the ACA would be implemented.

Decision 8: Allow Flexibility in Implementing the ACA Following Court Rulings and Initial Technical Hurdles

After Obama's second inauguration, numerous concerns about implementing the ACA became evident as the 1 October 2013 deadline neared for the opening of online health insurance exchanges where people could compare plans and sign up for coverage effective 1 January 2014. Problems included a lack of state health insurance exchanges; only about one-third of the states and the District of Columbia had created their own exchanges, leaving the federal government to establish and maintain an exchange for residents of other states (in partnership with a few states and completely independently for about half of them). In addition, given the Supreme Court's ruling that states could opt out of the ACA's Medicaid expansion, more than half of them planned to do so.

Plus there was the challenge of getting young Americans to comply with the health insurance mandate.[17]

The refusal by more than two-thirds of states to create their own health insurance exchanges demonstrated the power of federalism in American politics. As one scholar noted, states "recognize that they are in the driver's seat of healthcare reform," due to limited penalties for not meeting federal deadlines.[18] The Obama administration had expected people whose incomes fell below the poverty line to have access to health care through the ACA's expansion of Medicaid, but states that did not expand their Medicaid programs would not receive funding to cover "optional" populations or people who did not meet Medicaid eligibility requirements.[19] Surveys of young Americans found that they did not have extensive knowledge about the new health care law and were very concerned about cost.[20]

Further complicating the rollout of the online health insurance exchanges was the partial shutdown of the federal government on 1–16 October 2013 due to partisan conflict over the ACA. During budget negotiations for the 2014 fiscal year, which began on 1 October 2013, some congressional Republicans repeatedly tried to insert provisions to obstruct the ACA's implementation. In late September Senator Ted Cruz (R-TX) declared that he would speak on the Senate floor against the health care law "until I am no longer able to stand." He ultimately spoke for twenty-one hours, the fourth-longest speech in Senate history, interspersing critiques of the law with nongermane topics, such as reading Dr. Seuss's *Green Eggs and Ham* to his daughters, who were watching him on television.[21] The Democratic-led Senate would not pass the Republican-led House's budget legislation, which called for a one-year delay in the individual health insurance mandate and required executive and legislative employees to purchase health insurance through the new exchanges without any subsidies.[22] Ultimately, Congress and the president enacted budget legislation that included a minor change to the ACA, requiring income verification for people who received health insurance subsidies.[23]

Ending the government shutdown did not, however, solve the problems with the ACA's online portal, which stymied millions of individuals in the first few weeks. As the *New York Times* reported on 12 October, "a system costing more than $400 million and billed as a one-stop click-and-go hub for citizens seeking health insurance has thwarted the efforts of millions to simply log in. . . . The growing national outcry has deeply embarrassed the White House."[24] More than fourteen million people had visited the federal exchange by that date, but only a small number had been able to enroll in insurance plans, and several enrollees were notified of errors through the portal. Technological failures had been anticipated. Performance tests conducted just days before HealthCare.gov went live found that the website could not handle five hundred users at once. Not surprisingly, the website crashed shortly after it went online.[25]

In addition, of the approximately fourteen million Americans who carried individual health insurance because they did not have coverage through their employers, a significant number were informed that their policies might not be renewed because the plans did not meet ACA requirements.[26] This contradicted Obama's famous promise that "if you like your health-care plan, you'll be able to keep your health-care plan, period. No one will take it away, no matter what."[27] The ACA's requirement that insurers provide "essential health benefits" in ten categories, including prescription drugs, emergency care, and mental health services, disqualified several existing plans that provided limited coverage.

The ACA allowed some plans to be grandfathered into the new system, but strict implementation regulations, particularly very small permissible increases in copayments, prohibited the continuation of many individual plans.[28] One news organization declared that Obama's oft-repeated promise that people would be able to keep their health care plans was 2013's "lie of the year."[29] The Obama administration eventually announced that people whose plans were canceled would be given a "hardship exemption" from the insurance mandate, giving them more time to find a suitable policy. Additionally, the administration provided a temporary window for people to keep insurance plans that did not meet ACA requirements, if permitted by the insurers and the states. Ultimately, approximately 2.6 million people's individual health insurance plans were canceled due to noncompliance with the ACA.[30] Even though the number was lower than originally anticipated, the controversy complicated what was already a messy rollout for the ACA.[31]

Three weeks after the health exchange website went live, Obama addressed the numerous technical problems from the White House Rose Garden, saying, "No one is madder than me."[32] On a positive note, the administration cited the success of the website's data hub, which linked federal agencies to determine whether individuals were eligible for health care and subsidies through the ACA.[33] The Department of Health and Human Services requested assistance from tech experts inside and outside government to rectify the website issues. The White House also brought back former administration officials to address the rollout issues, including Jeffrey D. Zients (former acting OMB director) and Philip M. Schiliro (former White House director of legislative affairs).[34]

In the spring of 2014 Schiliro announced that implementation of the ACA was going well. More than five million Americans had registered for health insurance through the federal or state marketplaces, three million young Americans were receiving health insurance through parental coverage, and millions of people had confirmed their eligibility for either Medicaid or the Children's Health Insurance Program. The administration also released four hundred pages of guidance on health exchange and insurance standards for 2015 to give insurers more time to prepare for the next round of applications and enrollment.[35]

The Supreme Court Revisits the ACA

After overcoming its initial implementation difficulties, the ACA continued to face legal and political hurdles. A 2015 Supreme Court case addressed the constitutionality of tax credits for people who enrolled in a health insurance plan through the federal government's exchange. After Obama left office, a 2021 law repealed the individual mandate, which prompted another Supreme Court case that revisited the law's constitutionality. Although the ACA remained intact through these challenges, support for the law continued to be divided largely along party lines, even as the number of participants in the state and federal exchanges grew.

In *King v. Burwell* (2015) the Supreme Court examined whether individuals who purchased health insurance through a federally created or managed exchange were eligible to receive tax credits for their health care coverage. The ACA stated that health insurance tax credits, or subsidies, would be available to people who enrolled "through an Exchange established by the State."[36] Four Virginia residents filed a lawsuit based on this wording. Because the cost of their insurance premiums, with the tax credit, would be less than 8 percent of their income—the ACA's threshold for exemption from the individual mandate—they were forced to buy health insurance, even though they preferred not to. They argued that they were not eligible to receive the credit because Virginia used a federal exchange rather than a state exchange.[37]

Had the Supreme Court accepted this argument, more than six million Americans might have become ineligible for the health insurance tax credit. Instead, the Supreme Court ruled six to three that tax credits were permissible for people who purchased health insurance on a federal exchange. Chief Justice Roberts wrote the majority opinion, stating that although a literal reading of the statute apparently would not encompass a federal exchange, that interpretation "would destabilize the individual insurance market in any State with a Federal Exchange, and likely create the very 'death spirals' that Congress designed the Act to avoid. . . . A fair reading of legislation demands a fair understanding of the legislative plan."[38]

Opponents of the ACA subsequently took a legislative approach to undermining if not overturning the law. A signature issue in Donald Trump's 2016 presidential campaign was repeal of the ACA, and after his unexpected victory, he and the Republican-led 115th Congress attempted to do so. When those efforts failed, they pursued an indirect strategy with the 2017 Tax Cuts and Jobs Act, which removed the penalty for not having health insurance, effectively eliminating the individual mandate.[39] Soon after, some twenty states filed a federal lawsuit claiming that ending the individual mandate penalty removed a fundamental premise of the ACA, making the entire law unconstitutional. But in 2021 the Supreme Court ruled seven to two that the plaintiffs lacked standing because removing the penalty caused them no harm, thereby upholding the ACA once again.[40]

Conclusion

Despite the many legal and political challenges to the ACA, as well as the initial implementation issues, the law succeeded in expanding access to health care during the Obama presidency. The number of uninsured Americans dropped by almost 13 million, from 41.8 million in 2013 to 29 million in 2015. Coverage under private plans expanded due to subsidies to pay for health insurance, as well as young adults' ability to be covered by their parents' plans until age twenty-six. Coverage under public plans also increased due to the expansion of Medicaid in several states. The ACA's elimination of lifetime coverage limits also enabled people to receive long-term medical care that would have surpassed those limits.[41]

At both the five- and ten-year anniversaries of the law's passage, progress in expanding access to health insurance was clearly evident. As the *New York Times* wrote in 2015, "The verdict is indisputable: Its disastrous 2013 rollout notwithstanding, the Affordable Care Act has achieved nearly all its ambitious goals."[42] The creation of health insurance exchanges and subsidies, the expansion of Medicaid, and the establishment of minimum standards for insurance plans helped some thirty-one million Americans. Millions more benefited from the ACA provisions prohibiting the denial of coverage for preexisting conditions and permitting adult children to be covered by their parents' insurance until age twenty-six.[43] Ten years after Obama signed the ACA, some twenty million more Americans had health insurance, and racial, gender, and ethnic gaps in health care coverage had decreased. Among Black adults, there was a 10 percent drop in the number of people who lacked health insurance; for Hispanic adults, the percentage of uninsured dropped by more than one-third.[44]

Still, the ACA fell short of its ambitious goals. *Time* magazine described the law as "deeply flawed," citing the cost of health insurance as well as the difficulty of containing health care costs.[45] The Commonwealth Fund, an organization dedicated to improving health care in the United States, found that although the law significantly expanded access to health care, particularly for people of color and those with low incomes, its advances in other areas were more difficult to identify. As stated in a Commonwealth Fund report, "The law's effects on the cost and quality of health care services are difficult to discern given the complexity of our health system."[46] Health insurance remained largely out of reach for people who did not qualify for Medicaid or subsidies.

Another study concluded that although the ACA expanded access to health insurance, health care coverage did not necessarily improve. Furthermore, working-class and middle-class people who were ineligible for Medicaid lacked sufficient financial assistance to pay insurance premiums.[47] The ACA also permitted health insurance companies to set higher deductibles for people in the individual marketplace than those covered by employer-sponsored plans, creating a significant financial obstacle to health care even for the insured.[48] Future presidents would have to address the challenge of soaring health care costs.

Nevertheless, Obama's leadership in enacting the ACA resulted in the most significant expansion of health care since the creation of Medicare and Medicaid in 1965. Higher subsidies, through tax credits for people who signed up for health insurance through the ACA-created marketplaces, were enacted in the 2021 American Rescue Plan and renewed through 2025 by the 2022 Inflation Reduction Act, ensuring that recipients would continue to have access to affordable health care.[49] Subsequent debates have frequently recommended adding a public option for people not covered by the ACA—something Obama and Congress had considered and many Democrats viewed as a lost opportunity in 2010.[50] Even more comprehensive reform proposals, such as "Medicare for all" advocated by Senator Bernie Sanders of Vermont in the 2020 presidential campaign, recognize the ACA's foundational importance in providing affordable health care for millions of Americans.[51] Obama's landmark presidential decision created a path to health security that will potentially endure for generations.[52]

CONCLUSION

Assessing Obama's Leadership

President Obama's leadership was essential for achieving health care reform in 2010. Without his steadfast commitment to the issue, particularly after Democrats unexpectedly lost their filibuster-proof majority in the Senate, the Affordable Care Act almost certainly would not have been enacted that year. In addition to Obama's direct engagement in building political support for the legislation, senior White House staff and Democratic leaders in Congress skillfully orchestrated the bill's passage just fourteen months after Obama took office.

Despite Obama's success, controversies continued over the legislative process, key provisions of the ACA, and its implementation. The partisan divide over the merits of the ACA prompted debate over whether the president should have selected a less polarizing issue for his signature policy goal upon taking office. Obama's decision was consequential for Democrats in the 2010 midterm elections, when they lost control of the House by a significant margin. Substantively, Democrats and Republicans sharply disagreed on the merits of a health insurance mandate, the creation of marketplace exchanges where people could compare and select health insurance plans, the ACA's cost over time, and related topics. The rocky rollout of the marketplace exchanges in the fall of 2013 prompted further critiques of the Obama administration's management of health care reform.

Evaluating the eight presidential decisions that contributed to the ACA's passage illustrates Obama's successes and challenges in enacting the ACA.

Decision 1: Make a Firm Commitment to Health Care Reform in the 2008 Presidential Campaign

In many respects, this decision was not particularly notable, given the Democratic Party's long-standing commitment to health care reform. All the party's candidates for the nomination agreed on the pressing need to expand access to health care and reduce costs; their areas of disagreement centered on issues such as a health insurance mandate, which would require extensive negotiations with Congress. Obama's commitment to health care reform was important and consistent with Democratic policy priorities.

Decision 2: Identify Health Care Reform as an Immediate Priority in 2009

This decision was highly significant, as Obama had multiple options for the top spot on his agenda, from the financial crisis to climate change to immigration policy. Given how polarizing the health care debate quickly became, some scholars and policymakers questioned whether the president should have deferred action on health care and focused on another issue that was more likely to garner bipartisan support. Obama's perseverance on health care reform was essential to enacting the ACA slightly more than a year after he took office. Furthermore, Obama expected White House and executive branch officials active in health care reform to devote their full energy to fulfilling this goal, and he made it clear that he valued their dedication, expertise, and contributions. As Jeanne Lambrew, who served as director of the Office of Health Reform in the Department of Health and Human Services, said:

> Any first year of an administration is rough and tumble. . . . And yet, [Obama] was able to, through his leadership skills, his own set of expectations of all of us, have a civil, inclusive, and respectful environment. . . . If you were at the table, you were heard, whether you wanted to speak or not, because you were there for a reason. And his . . . expectation of all of us to be the best people we could

be, was something that I am convinced not only created the kind of shared commitment to the policy goals that he achieved but made all of us better people.[1]

Decision 3: Exercise White House Leadership to Start the Policymaking Process for Health Care Reform in the Spring of 2009

To ensure that health care reform would move forward, Obama's initiative in starting the policymaking process in the spring of 2009 was crucial. Bringing health care experts, analysts, lobbyists, and legislators to the White House to discuss how to balance expanded access to health care and manageable costs set the stage for subsequent executive-legislative debates. Without leadership from the White House, health care reform might have been delayed to deal with more pressing policy issues. Additionally, Obama's attentiveness to the many components of health care reform was essential to the development of a comprehensive legislative plan, despite obstacles encountered along the way. As White House adviser Nancy-Ann DeParle later reflected, Obama presented the challenge like a Rubik's cube: "We've just got to get [all the moving parts] into place." Throughout the legislative process, DeParle said, "There were a lot of days . . . where you get two things to agree, and then the other one would be a problem."[2]

Decision 4: Defer to Congress to Develop Health Care Legislation in the Summer of 2009

Although executive leadership was needed to start the policymaking process for health care reform, Obama appreciated the importance of Congress taking the lead in developing legislation. Deep congressional engagement was essential to building coalitions in the House and Senate. Additionally, bipartisan efforts in each chamber showed early promise, albeit with unfulfilled expectations.

Decision 5: Refocus Legislative Efforts on Health Care Reform in the Fall of 2009

After a tumultuous summer of legislative debates on Capitol Hill and public critiques in town hall meetings designed to build support for health care reform, Obama recognized the need to reset the conversation in September 2009. By delivering a special message to Congress focused on health care reform, Obama made it clear that he would press forward and that advocates of reform should do the same. While Obama's speech and subsequent White House negotiations did not succeed in building a bipartisan coalition, they led to the House and Senate passing their own versions of reform legislation by the end of 2009.

Decision 6: Continue to Advance Health Care Reform after the Democrats Lose Their Filibuster-Proof Senate Majority in January 2010

After the stunning upset in the Massachusetts special election that resulted in the Democrats losing their filibuster-proof majority in the Senate, prospects for health care reform appeared to be greatly diminished, if not doomed. But Obama did not waver in his determination to move forward from the House and Senate bills passed in November and December 2009, respectively. Instead of following the traditional legislative path of finding common ground between the two bills via conference committee, Obama was willing to employ a special procedure to achieve his policy goal. And the president was deeply involved in the process. As Secretary of Health and Human Services Kathleen Sebelius later said, "He was negotiator in chief. . . . The President of the United States not only knew what was in the House bill and the Senate bill; he knew all of the areas where there were differences. He could walk through each of the issues, and he did."[3]

Decision 7: Enact the ACA through the Budgetary Process of Reconciliation in March 2010

Obama's decision to work with the House to pass the Senate bill and then enact health care reform through the reconciliation process allowed him to follow through on his campaign pledge within the promised time frame. Collaborating closely with congressional leaders, particularly Speaker Nancy Pelosi, the Obama White House succeeded in gaining House support for the Senate bill, albeit with some modifications that would be passed separately. Although the ACA passed on a party-line vote, and the law would continue to be a polarizing issue long after its passage, Obama was able to achieve success.

Decision 8: Allow Flexibility in Implementing the ACA Following Court Rulings and Initial Technical Hurdles

The Obama administration faced multiple logistical and technological hurdles related to implementing the ACA, but it also demonstrated a clear learning curve in responding to events. After a shaky rollout in the fall of 2013, Obama brought in two special advisers to improve access to the online federal insurance marketplace and address other operational issues. By the time Obama left office in 2017, the ACA's major provisions to expand access to health care were functioning as envisioned. Still, the many components of health care reform were difficult to institute and explain. According to Elizabeth Fowler, chief counsel to Senate Finance Committee chair Max Baucus and an official in the Obama administration, "The ACA was a complicated bill building on a complicated healthcare system. In trying to preserve as much of the underlying coverage as possible, you just add to the complexity."[4]

For Obama, enacting the ACA in March 2010 fulfilled a major campaign promise to expand access to health care for Americans at a manageable cost. Since then, the law has endured multiple court challenges and has undergone some notable changes—particularly the Supreme Court's 2012 decision that the ACA could not mandate the states' expansion of Medicaid and the 2017 repeal of the individual mandate by President Donald Trump and the 115th Congress. Still, the ACA's endurance through three presidencies, including two years of unified government in the White House and Congress by the party that uniformly opposed the law, demonstrates its success.

At the same time, the political polarization that has persisted since the ACA's enactment is also part of Obama's leadership legacy. When it became clear that there was no chance of winning Republican support for his health care reform proposal, the president forged ahead to build Democratic coalitions on Capitol Hill to pass the law. Subsequent assessments of the ACA have largely followed party lines, with Democrats praising the law's expansion of access to health care and Republicans criticizing costs and the multiple requirements for individuals, states, and health insurance companies under the law. A bipartisan law would have had a stronger foundation for public and governing support, but to Obama, passing a law without bipartisanship was preferable to not passing a law at all.

Future presidents can learn from Obama's leadership in agenda setting, policy negotiations, and commitment to achieving stated policy goals. The limits of partisan leadership notwithstanding, broader forces of polarization in American politics may make bipartisanship an insurmountable bar for many issues, at least in the near future. The substance of the ACA is also subject to ongoing debate, and additional changes to the American health care system will likely be proposed in the coming years. When that happens, Obama's successors will study his leadership in enacting the ACA to decide how to pursue their own policy priorities.

NOTES

INTRODUCTION: OBAMA'S LEADERSHIP ON HEALTH CARE REFORM

1. As discussed in chapters 3 and 4, thirty-nine Democrats voted against the House bill in November 2009, and forty-five Democrats voted against the final legislation in March 2010. In the Senate, the entire Democratic caucus voted for the bill, although the Democrats had to use a special procedure to enact the legislation after losing their filibuster-proof majority in January 2010. Jonathan Allen, "Only 3 of 45 House Democrats Who Voted 'No' on Obamacare Are Still There," Vox, 1 September 2015, www.vox.com; "Obamacare Overview," www.ballotpedia.org.

2. Harry S. Truman, "Special Message to the Congress Recommending a Comprehensive Health Program," 19 November 1945, Harry S. Truman Library and Museum, https://www.trumanlibrary.gov/library/public-papers/192/special-message-congress-recommending-comprehensive-health-program.

3. Lyndon B. Johnson, "Remarks with President Truman at the Signing in Independence of the Medicare Bill," 30 July 1965, LBJ Presidential Library, http://www.lbjlibrary.net/collections/selected-speeches/1965/07-30-1965.html.

4. William J. Clinton, "Address to a Joint Session of Congress on Health Care Reform," 22 September 1993, Gerhard Peters and John T. Woolley, American Presidency Project, https://www.presidency.ucsb.edu/node/217830.

5. Glenn Thrush and Carrie Budoff Brown, "Obama's Health Care Conversion," *Politico*, 22 September 2013, https://www.politico.com/story/2013/09/obama-health-care-conversion-obamacare-097185.

6. George C. Edwards III, *Predicting the Presidency: The Potential of Persuasive Leadership* (Princeton, NJ: Princeton University Press, 2016), 44–45, 208–209.

7. Physicians for a National Health Program, "A Brief History: Universal Health Care Efforts in the US," https://pnhp.org/a-brief-history-universal-health-care-efforts-in-the-us/.

8. Edward S. Corwin, *The President: Office and Powers* (New York: NYU/George Grady Press, 1940); Clinton Rossiter, *The American Presidency: The Powers and Practices, the Personalities and Problems of the Most Important Office in the World* (New York: Harcourt, Brace, 1956).

9. Arthur M. Schlesinger Sr., "Historians Rate U.S. Presidents," *Life*, 1 November 1948; Arthur M. Schlesinger Jr., "Rating the Presidents: Washington to Clinton," *Political Science Quarterly* 112, 2 (Summer 1997): 179–190. In the last few decades, many scholars and news organizations have developed presidential ratings surveys; selected surveys are discussed in Meena Bose and Mark Landis, eds., *The Uses and Abuses of Presidential Ratings* (Hauppauge, NY: Nova Science Publishers, 2003). A 2018 survey by political scientists is examined in Brandon Rottinghaus, Gregory Eady, and Justin S. Vaughn, "Presidential Greatness in a Polarized Era: Results from the Latest Presidential Greatness Survey," *PS:*

Political Science & Politics 53, 3 (2020): 413–420. Rottinghaus and Vaughn published a new survey, "Official Results of the 2024 Presidential Greatness Project Expert Survey," in February 2024, which is available at http://www.brandonrottinghaus.com/uploads/1/0/8/7/108798321/presidential_greatness_white_paper_2024.pdf.

10. Richard E. Neustadt, *Presidential Power: The Politics of Leadership* (New York: John Wiley & Sons, 1960). Neustadt's classic study has been updated several times to add chapters on subsequent presidents; the last expanded edition is *Presidential Power and the Modern Presidents* (New York: Free Press, 1990).

11. Fred I. Greenstein, *The Presidential Difference: Leadership Style from Roosevelt to Clinton* (New York: Free Press, 2000). The latest edition is *The Presidential Difference: Leadership Style from FDR to Barack Obama*, 3rd ed. (Princeton, NJ: Princeton University Press, 2009).

12. Adam Nagourney and Jeff Zeleny, "Obama Formally Enters Presidential Race," *New York Times*, 11 February 2007.

13. James P. Pfiffner, *The Strategic Presidency: Hitting the Ground Running*, 2nd rev. ed. (Lawrence: University Press of Kansas, 1996), 112.

14. Paul C. Light, *The President's Agenda: Domestic Policy Choice from Kennedy to Carter*, 3rd ed. (Baltimore: Johns Hopkins University Press, 1998).

15. Partnership for Public Service, Center for Presidential Transition, "How Bush and Obama Created a Gold Standard Transition," 7 November 2020, https://presidentialtransition.org/publications/how-bush-and-obama-created-a-gold-standard-transition/. For example, National Security Council experts in the Bush administration prepared a series of foreign policy memoranda for Obama's national security team. These are published with commentary in Stephen J. Hadley, Peter D. Feaver, William C. Inboden, and Meghan L. O'Sullivan, eds., *Hand-off: The Foreign Policy George W. Bush Passed to Barack Obama* (Washington, DC: Brookings Institution Press, 2023).

16. Martha Joynt Kumar, "Presidential Transition through the Voices of Its Participants," *Presidential Studies Quarterly* 39, 4 (December 2009): 857. Also see Martha Joynt Kumar, *Before the Oath: How George W. Bush and Barack Obama Managed a Transfer of Power* (Baltimore: Johns Hopkins University Press, 2015).

17. Klaus Marre, "Obama Praises Bush for Smooth Transition," *Hill*, 17 January 2009.

18. Representative sources include John P. Burke and Fred I. Greenstein with Larry Berman and Richard Immerman, *How Presidents Test Reality: Decisions on Vietnam, 1954 and 1965* (New York: Russell Sage Foundation, 1989); John P. Burke, *The Institutional Presidency* (Baltimore: Johns Hopkins University Press, 1992); Charles E. Walcott and Karen M. Hult, *Governing the White House: From Hoover through LBJ* (Lawrence: University Press of Kansas, 1995); Daniel Ponder, *Good Advice: Information and Policy Making in the White House* (College Station: Texas A&M University Press, 2000); Stephen Hess and James P. Pfiffner, *Organizing the Presidency*, 3rd ed. (Washington, DC: Brookings Institution Press, 2002).

19. The classic study that provides the scholarly foundation for numerous works on the American presidency taking this approach is Terry Moe, "The Polit-

icized Presidency," in *The New Direction in American Politics*, ed. John E. Chubb and Paul E. Peterson (Washington, DC: Brookings Institution, 1985). Scholarship that builds on this analysis includes Thomas J. Weko, *The Politicizing Presidency: The White House Personnel Office, 1948–1994* (Lawrence: University Press of Kansas, 1995); and Daniel Galvin and Colleen Shogan, "Presidential Politicization and Centralization across the Modern-Traditional Divide," *Polity* 36, 3 (April 2004): 477–504.

20. Only a small sample of the excellent and original scholarship on these topics is included here. More extensive bibliographies are available in many textbooks on the American presidency, including Thomas E. Cronin, Michael A. Genovese, and Meena Bose, *The Paradoxes of the American Presidency*, 6th ed. (New York: Oxford University Press, 2022); George C. Edwards III, Kenneth R. Mayer, and Stephen J. Wayne, *Presidential Leadership: Politics and Policy Making*, 12th ed. (New York: Rowman & Littlefield, 2022); Lori Cox Han and Diane J. Heith, *Presidents and the American Presidency*, 3rd ed. (New York: Oxford University Press, 2022); Sidney M. Milkis and Michael Nelson, *The American Presidency: Origins and Development, 1776–2021*, 9th ed. (Washington, DC: CQ Press, 2022).

21. Barack H. Obama cabinet nominations, https://www.senate.gov/legislative/nominations/Obama_cabinet.htm.

22. James P. Pfiffner, "Decision Making in the Obama White House," *Presidential Studies Quarterly* 41, 2 (June 2011): 260, 261.

23. See, for example, Samuel Kernell, *Going Public: New Strategies of Presidential Leadership*, 4th ed. (Washington, DC: CQ Press, 2006); George C. Edwards III, *At the Margins: Presidential Leadership of Congress* (New Haven, CT: Yale University Press, 1990); Andrew Rudalevige, *Managing the President's Program: Presidential Leadership and Legislative Policy Formulation* (Princeton, NJ: Princeton University Press, 2002); John P. Burke, *Presidential Power: Theories and Dilemmas* (New York: Routledge, 2019).

24. The classic study of US policymaking from the late twentieth to early twenty-first centuries is John W. Kingdon, *Agendas, Alternatives, and Public Policies*, updated 2nd ed., with epilogue on health care reform (New York: Longman, 2011). A recent study that applies Kingdon's concept of "policy streams" to passage of the ACA is James M. Brasfield, *The Affordable Care Act: At the Nexus of Politics and Policy* (Boulder, CO: Lynne Rienner, 2022).

25. John Weinberg, "The Great Recession and Its Aftermath," Federal Reserve, www.federalreservehistory.org.

26. Kingdon, *Agendas, Alternatives, and Public Policies*, 247.

27. Lydia Saad, "By Slim Margins, Americans Support Healthcare Bill's Passage," Gallup, 23 March 2010.

28. Cronin, Genovese, and Bose, *Paradoxes of the American Presidency*.

29. James MacGregor Burns, *Leadership* (New York: HarperCollins, 1978), 4.

30. Robin Givhan, "Mussed for Success: Barack Obama's Smooth Wrinkles," *Washington Post*, 11 August 2006, cited in Stanley Renshon, "Unfulfilled Hopes: President Obama's Legacy," in *Looking Back on President Barack Obama's Legacy: Hope and Change*, ed. Wilbur C. Rich (New York: Palgrave Macmillan, 2019), 211–248.

31. Tim Russert, *Meet the Press* interview transcript, NBC, 22 October 2008, cited in Renshon, "Unfulfilled Hopes," 216–217.

32. See Fred I. Greenstein, "Can Personality and Politics Be Studied Systematically?" *Political Psychology* 13, 1 (March 1992): 105–128, for a discussion of how to identify when actors themselves, not just their actions, are key to a policy outcome ("action dispensability" versus "actor dispensability").

33. "Exclusive: Obama Would 'Rather Be Really Good One-Term President,'" ABC News, 25 January 2010, www.abcnewsgo.com.

34. Renshon, "Unfulfilled Hopes," 219.

35. See, for example, Pfiffner, *Strategic Presidency*; Light, *President's Agenda*. Jeff Fishel, *Presidents and Promises: From Campaign Pledge to Presidential Performance* (Washington, DC: CQ Press, 1985), is also instructive on this topic.

36. A cogent analysis of the sources and consequences of deepening political divisions in American politics is Ezra Klein, *Why We're Polarized* (New York: Simon & Schuster, 2020).

37. Morris P. Fiorina, *Unstable Majorities: Polarization, Party Sorting, and Political Stalemate* (Stanford, CA: Hoover Institution Press, 2017); Alan I. Abramowitz, *The Great Alignment: Race, Party Transformation, and the Rise of Donald Trump* (New Haven, CT: Yale University Press, 2018); Lilliana Mason, *Uncivil Agreement: How Politics Became Our Identity* (Chicago: University of Chicago Press, 2018).

CHAPTER 1. HOW DID HEALTH CARE BECOME A PUBLIC POLICY PRIORITY?

1. James M. Brasfield, *The Affordable Care Act: At the Nexus of Politics and Policy* (Boulder, CO: Lynne Rienner, 2022), 4.

2. "U.S. History Primary Source Timeline: Progressive Era to New Era, 1900–1929—Overview," Library of Congress, https://www.loc.gov/classroom-ma terials/united-states-history-primary-source-timeline/progressive-era-to-new -era-1900-1929/overview/; "Public Health in the Progressive Era," Oregon Health and Science University Historical Collections and Archives, https://www.ohsu .edu/historical-collections-archives/public-health-progressive-era.

3. For a comprehensive study of the evolution of American health care from the mid-eighteenth to late twentieth centuries, see Paul Starr, *The Social Transformation of American Medicine* (New York: Basic Books, 1982).

4. "Professionalization of Public Health," Oregon Health and Science University Historical Collections and Archives, https://www.ohsu.edu/historical -collections-archives/professionalization-public-health.

5. Beatrix Hoffman, "Health Care Reform and Social Movements in the United States," *American Journal of Public Health* 93, 1 (January 2003): 75–85; Brasfield, *Affordable Care Act*, 4.

6. Roosevelt had previously served almost two full terms as president. As vice president, he assumed the presidency following the assassination of William McKinley in 1901 and then won election in 1904. He did not run for reelection in

1908 and became the Progressive Party candidate after failing to win the Republican nomination in 1912.

7. Anne-Emmanuelle Birn, Theodore M. Brown, Elizabeth Fee, and Walter J. Lear, "Struggles for National Health Reform in the United States," *American Journal of Public Health* 93, 1 (January 2003): 86–91; Clifford Marks, "Inside the American Medical Association's Fight over Single-Payer Health Care," *New Yorker*, 22 February 2022.

8. Howard L. Reiter, "The Bases of Progressivism within the Major Parties: Evidence from the National Conventions," *Social Science History* 22, 1 (Spring 1998): 83–116; Robert T. Johnston, "Re-Democratizing the Progressive Era: The Politics of Progressive Era Political Historiography," *Journal of the Gilded Age and Progressive Era* 1, 1 (January 2002): 68–92; Hoffman, "Health Care Reform."

9. Birn et al., "Struggles for National Health Reform"; Hoffman, "Health Care Reform."

10. Harry S. Truman, "Special Message to the Congress Recommending a Comprehensive Health Program," 19 November 1945, Harry S. Truman Library and Museum.

11. Harry S. Truman, "Radio Report to the American People on the Status of the Reconversion Program," 3 January 1946, Gerhard Peters and John T. Woolley, American Presidency Project, https://www.presidency.ucsb.edu/node/232009; "7 Times Harry Truman Made the Case for National Health Care," Truman Library Institute, https://www.trumanlibraryinstitute.org/health-care/; Monte Poen, *Harry S. Truman versus the Medical Lobby: The Genesis of Medicare* (Columbia: University of Missouri Press, 1979).

12. 1948 Democratic Party Platform, Peters and Woolley, American Presidency Project, https://www.presidency.ucsb.edu/node/273225.

13. William E. Leuchtenberg, "New Faces of 1946," *Smithsonian Magazine*, November 2006, https://www.smithsonianmag.com/history/new-faces-of-1946-135190660/.

14. Jonathan Oberlander, "Lessons from the Long and Winding Road to Medicare for All," *American Journal of Public Health* 109, 11 (2019): 1497–1500.

15. Christian N. J. Roberts, "Dynamics of Healthcare Reform: Bitter Pills Old and New," *Vanderbilt Journal of Transnational Law* 45, 5 (November 2012): 1341–1380.

16. Lyndon B. Johnson, "Address before a Joint Session of the Congress," 27 November 1963, Peters and Woolley, American Presidency Project, https://www.presidency.ucsb.edu/node/238734.

17. Lyndon B. Johnson, "Annual Message to the Congress on the State of the Union," 8 January 1964, Peters and Woolley, American Presidency Project, https://www.presidency.ucsb.edu/node/242292.

18. John Dickerson, "Kennedycare: Fifty Years before Obamacare, JFK Had His Own Health Care Debacle," Slate, 17 November 2013, https://slate.com/news-and-politics/2013/11/john-f-kennedys-health-care-failure-jfk-and-barack-obamas-tough-fights-to-reform-health-care.html.

19. John F. Kennedy, "Address on Support of Medicare," New York, 20 May 1962, https://www.historycentral.com/JFK/Speeches/Medicare.html.

20. Quoted in Paul Starr, *Remedy and Reaction: The Peculiar American Struggle over Health Care Reform* (New Haven, CT: Yale University Press, 2011), 45.

21. Starr, *Social Transformation of American Medicine*, 366–369.

22. Lyndon B. Johnson, "Annual Message to Congress on the State of the Union," 4 January 1965, Peters and Woolley, American Presidency Project, https://www.presidency.ucsb.edu/node/241819; US House of Representatives, History, Art, and Archives, "President Johnson's 1965 State of the Union Address," https://history.house.gov/Collection/Listing/2009/2009-016-008/.

23. *US House of Representatives, History, Art, and Archives,* "89th Congress (1965–1967)," https://history.house.gov/Congressional-Overview/Profiles/89th/.

24. Starr, *Remedy and Reaction*, 44–46. Also see Paul Starr, "The Health Care Legacy of the Great Society," in *LBJ's Neglected Legacy: How Lyndon Johnson Reshaped Domestic Policy and Government*, ed. Robert H. Wilson, Norman J. Glickman, and Laurence E. Lynn Jr. (Austin: University Press of Texas, 2015); Brasfield, *Affordable Care Act*, 11.

25. Social Security Administration, Legislative History, "Vote Tallies for Passage of Medicare in 1965," https://www.ssa.gov/history/tally65.html.

26. "Medicare and Medicaid Act," Lyndon B. Johnson Presidential Library, https://www.lbjlibrary.org/news-and-press/media-kits/medicare-and-medicaid; Howard Markel, "How Medicare Came to Be, Thanks to Harry S. Truman," *PBS NewsHour*, 30 July 2014, https://www.pbs.org/newshour/health/president-johnson-signs-medicare-law.

27. See David Blumenthal and James Morone, *The Heart of Power, with a New Preface: Health and Politics in the Oval Office* (Berkeley: University of California Press, 2010), 163–205, for an assessment of Johnson's influential leadership in creating the Medicare and Medicaid programs.

28. See Kaiser Family Foundation, "Timeline: History of Health Reform in the U.S.," for an instructive summary of proposals and actions on health care policy from the early twentieth century to passage of the Affordable Care Act in 2010.

29. David W. Brady and Daniel P. Kessler, "Why Is Health Reform So Difficult?" *Journal of Health Politics, Policy and Law* 35, 2 (April 2010): 161–175.

30. David Maraniss, *First in His Class: The Biography of Bill Clinton* (New York: Touchstone, 1995), 461–462.

31. Bill Clinton, "Announcement Speech," Old State House, Little Rock, Arkansas, 3 October 1991, http://www.4president.org/speeches/billclinton1992announcement.htm.

32. Edward Luce, "U.S. Democrats Should Remember, 'It's the Economy, Stupid,'" *Financial Times*, 27 March 2019, https://www.ft.com/content/b8e4f7c8-5070-11e9-9c76-bf4a0ce37d49.

33. Adam Clymer, Robert Pear, and Robin Toner, "The Health Care Debate: What Went Wrong? How the Health Care Campaign Collapsed—A Special Report," *New York Times*, 29 August 1994.

34. "Health Care Reform Initiative," Clinton Digital Library, https://clinton.presidentiallibraries.us/health-reform-initiative.

35. Robert Pear, "Ending Its Secrecy, White House Lists Health-Care Panel," *New York Times*, 27 March 1993.

36. History.com editors, "Hillary Rodham Clinton," 9 November 2009, updated 25 February 2021, https://www.history.com/topics/first-ladies/hillary-rodham-clinton; Carl Bernstein, *A Woman in Charge: The Life of Hillary Rodham Clinton* (New York: Knopf Doubleday, 2008).

37. Robert Pear, "Court Rules that First Lady Is 'De Facto' Federal Official," *New York Times*, 23 June 1993.

38. David Gergen, *Eyewitness to Power: The Essence of Leadership, Nixon to Clinton* (New York: Touchstone, 2000), 307–308.

39. Blumenthal and Morone, *Heart of Power*, 368.

40. "Clinton's Health Plan: Transcript of President's Address to Congress on Health Care," *New York Times*, 23 September 1993, https://www.nytimes.com/1993/09/23/us/clinton-s-health-plan-transcript-president-s-address-congress-health-care.html; Elizabeth Drew, *On the Edge: The Clinton Presidency* (New York: Simon & Schuster, 1994), 300–303.

41. Dana Priest, "Health Care Testimony from the Top," *Washington Post*, 29 September 1993, https://www.washingtonpost.com/archive/politics/1993/09/29/health-care-testimony-from-the-top/a6079a40-d83e-4697-a5a1-9ad188b34174/.

42. Robert Pear, "Clinton's Health Plan: The Overview; Congress Is Given Clinton's Proposal for Health Care," *New York Times*, 28 October 1993, https://www.nytimes.com/1993/10/28/us/clinton-s-health-plan-overview-congress-given-clinton-proposal-for-health-care.html; H.R. 3600, 103rd Congress, 1st session, 20 November 1993, https://www.congress.gov/103/bills/hr3600/BILLS-103hr3600ih.pdf.

43. Blumenthal and Morone, *Heart of Power*, 371–372; "'Harry and Louise' Health Care Advertisements," C-SPAN, 10 July 1994.

44. Drew, *On the Edge*, 194.

45. Blumenthal and Morone, *Heart of Power*, 372–381.

46. Philip A. Klinkner, *Midterm: The Elections of 1994 in Context* (Boulder, CO: Westview Press, 1996).

47. Todd S. Purdum, "Undertones of Relevance," *New York Times*, 20 April 1995.

48. For recollections by Clinton administration officials about how the president prevailed in the battle with congressional Republicans over two government shutdowns, see Bryan Craig, "The 1995–96 Government Shutdown," Miller Center, University of Virginia, https://millercenter.org/1995-96-government-shutdown.

49. Todd S. Purdum, "Clinton Signs Bill to Give Portability in Insurance," *New York Times*, 22 August 1996.

50. Brasfield, *Affordable Care Act*, 23–24.

51. Blumenthal and Morone, *Heart of Power*, 381–384.

52. Gergen, *Eyewitness to Power*, 306–309.

53. Stanley A. Renshon, *High Hopes: The Clinton Presidency and the Politics of Ambition* (New York: Routledge, 1998), xi–xiii.

54. Joe Klein, *The Natural: The Misunderstood Presidency of Bill Clinton* (New York: Doubleday, 2002), 119–126.

55. Klein, 127, 130.

CHAPTER 2. WHY DID OBAMA MAKE HEALTH CARE REFORM A CAMPAIGN PROMISE IN 2008?

1. For an explanation of the concept of "policy streams" and its applicability to Obama's passage of the ACA, see Kingdon, *Agendas, Alternatives, and Public Policies*. Also see Ann-Laure Beaussier, "The Patient Protection and Affordable Care Act: The Victory of Unorthodox Lawmaking," *Journal of Health Politics, Policy and Law* 37, 5 (2012): 741–778; Brasfield, *Affordable Care Act*.

2. Informative biographies of Obama's early years include David Garrow, *Rising Star: The Making of Barack Obama* (New York: William Morrow, 2017); David Maraniss, *Barack Obama: The Story* (New York: Simon & Schuster, 2013); Michael Nelson, "Barack Obama: Life before the Presidency," Miller Center, University of Virginia, https://millercenter.org/president/obama/life-before-the-presidency; David Remnick, *The Bridge: The Life and Rise of Barack Obama* (New York: Random House, 2010).

3. Barack Obama, *Dreams from My Father: A Story of Race and Inheritance* (New York: Crown, 1995), 73, Kindle.

4. Obama, 80–107.

5. Obama, 75.

6. Martin Kaste, "Hawaii Prep School Gave Obama Window to Success," National Public Radio, 12 October 2012.

7. Larry Gordon, "Occidental Recalls 'Barry' Obama," *Los Angeles Times*, 29 January 2007.

8. Janny Scott, "Obama's Account of New York Years Often Differs from What Others Say," *New York Times*, 30 October 2007.

9. Scott.

10. David Mendell, *Obama: From Promise to Power* (New York: Amistad, 2007), quoted in Nelson, "Barack Obama: Life before the Presidency."

11. Serge Kovaleski, "Obama's Organizing Years, Guiding Others and Finding Himself," *New York Times*, 7 July 2008.

12. Obama, *Dreams from My Father*, 426.

13. Marie C. Kodama, "Obama Left Mark on HLS," *Harvard Crimson*, 19 January 2007.

14. Kodama.

15. Kodama.

16. Fox Butterfield, "First Black Elected to Head Harvard's Law Review," *New York Times*, 6 February 1990.

17. Deanna Janes, "A Timeline of Barack and Michelle Obama's Marriage," *Oprah Daily*, 8 September 2020; "First Lady Michelle Obama," Barack Obama Presidential Library.

18. Valerie Jarrett, *Finding My Voice: My Journey to the West Wing and the Path Forward* (New York: Viking, 2019), 107, 112.
19. Janny Scott, "The Story of Obama, Written by Obama," *New York Times*, 18 May 2008; Jodi Kantor, "Teaching Law, Testing Ideas, Obama Stood Slightly Apart," *New York Times*, 30 July 2008.
20. Gretchen Reynolds, "Vote of Confidence," *Chicago Magazine*, 1 May 1993.
21. Kevin Sack, "Book Challenges Obama on Mother's Deathbed Fight," *New York Times*, 13 July 2011; Janny Scott, *A Singular Woman: The Untold Story of Barack Obama's Mother* (New York: Riverhead Books, 2011).
22. Nelson, "Barack Obama: Life before the Presidency"; Drew Griffin and Kathleen Johnson, "Obama Played Hardball in First Chicago Campaign," 29 May 2008, Election Center 2008, https://www.cnn.com/2008/POLITICS/05/29/obamas.first.campaign/.
23. Janny Scott, "In Illinois, Obama Proved Pragmatic and Shrewd," *New York Times*, 30 July 2007; Sarah Zimmerman, "Illinois Debates Effectiveness of Racial Profile Data," APNews.com, 28 April 2018.
24. Scott, "In Illinois, Obama Proved Pragmatic."
25. Janny Scott, "In 2000, a Streetwise Veteran Schooled a Bold Young Obama," *New York Times*, 9 September 2007.
26. Michelle Obama, *Becoming* (New York: Crown, 2018), 269, 294, Kindle.
27. Quoted in Amy Davidson Sorkin, "Michelle Obama and Politics: A (Sort of) Love Story," *New Yorker*, 27 December 2018.
28. Caroline Kenny, "Obama's Other DNC Moment: His Credit Card Got Declined," 27 December 2016, www.cnn.com.
29. Scott, "In 2000, Streetwise Veteran Schooled."
30. John Mercurio, "Fitzgerald Announces He Won't Seek Second Term in Senate," 15 April 2003, www.cnn.com.
31. Christopher Drew and Mike McIntire, "After 2000 Loss, Obama Built Donor Network from Roots Up," *New York Times*, 3 April 2007.
32. "How Obama Has Benefited from Sex Scandals," *Newsweek*, 26 June 2009.
33. Dayo Olopade, "Barack's Big Night," *New Republic*, 25 August 2008; Todd Leopold, "The Day America Met Barack Obama," 5 November 2008, https://edition.cnn.com/2008/POLITICS/11/05/obama.meeting/index.html. Also see Mendell, *Obama: From Promise to Power*, for Obama's political career in Illinois and journey to the 2008 presidential campaign.
34. David Bernstein, "The Speech," *Chicago Magazine*, 29 May 2007.
35. "Barack Obama's Remarks to the Democratic National Convention," *New York Times*, 27 July 2004.
36. Robin Toner and Katharine Q. Seelye, "Convention Star Obama Wins Illinois Senate Seat," *New York Times*, 3 November 2004.
37. John Chase, David Mendell, and *Tribune* staff reporters, "Obama Sails to Senate Win," *Chicago Tribune*, 3 November 2004.
38. Kate Zernike and Jeff Zeleny, "Obama in Senate: Star Power, Minor Role," *New York Times*, 9 March 2008; Daniel Vock, "Obama: He Puts Ethics on the

Agenda," NPR Illinois, 1 February 2007; Chris Frates, "Congress Passes Ethics Reform Bill," *Politico*, 2 August 2007.

39. Manu Raju, "Book Disputes Reid's Obama Timeline," *Politico*, 10 January 2010.

40. Glenn Thrush and Carrie Budoff Brown, "Obama's Health Care Conversion," *Politico*, 22 September 2013.

41. "Full Text of Obama's Candidacy Speech," *Denver Post*, 10 February 2007.

42. Beaussier, "Patient Protection and Affordable Care Act," 749; Daniel Beland, Philip Rocco, and Alex Waddan, *Obamacare Wars: Federalism, State Politics, and the Affordable Care Act* (Lawrence: University Press of Kansas, 2016), 5–8, 42.

43. Beland et al., *Obamacare Wars*, 6.

44. Associated Press, "Is Obama All Style and Little Substance?" 27 March 2007, http://www.nbcnews.com.

45. Thrush and Brown, "Obama's Health Care Conversion."

46. Robin Toner, "2008 Candidates Vow to Overhaul U.S. Health Care," *New York Times*, 6 July 2007.

47. Toner. Also see Commonwealth Fund, "Envisioning the Future: The 2008 Presidential Candidates' Health Reform Proposals," 1 January 2008; Brasfield, *Affordable Care Act*, 36.

48. Matt Bai, "The Fallback," *New York Times Magazine*, 12 March 2006.

49. Ryan Lizza, "How to Beat Hillary Clinton," *New Yorker*, 13 October 2015; Catherine Garcia, "2007 Obama Campaign Memo Detailing How to Defeat Hillary Clinton Surfaces," *Week*, 13 October 2015.

50. Adam Nagourney and Jeff Zeleny, "Obama and Clinton Duel for Iowa Democrats," *New York Times*, 11 November 2007; Roger Simon, "Jefferson Jackson a Warm-up for Iowa," *Politico*, 11 November 2007.

51. Barack Obama, speech at Jefferson-Jackson dinner, Veterans Memorial Auditorium, Des Moines, IA, 10 November 2007.

52. Ana Marie Cox, "Can Obama Rock the Nomination?" *Time*, 11 November 2007.

53. Adam Nagourney, "Obama Takes Iowa in a Big Turnout as Clinton Falters; Huckabee Victor," *New York Times*, 4 January 2008.

54. "Election 2008: Primary Season Election Results," *New York Times*, 6 December 2016, https://archive.nytimes.com/www.nytimes.com/elections/2008/primaries/results/states/NY.html; Jeff Zeleny and Jennifer Steinhauer, "Clinton Defeats Obama in Nevada," *New York Times*, 19 January 2008.

55. Jeff Zeleny and Carl Hulse, "Kennedy Chooses Obama, Spurning Plea by Clintons," *New York Times*, 28 January 2008.

56. Brian Knowlton, "Senator Edward Kennedy Endorses Barack Obama," *New York Times*, 28 January 2008.

57. Caroline Kennedy, "A President Like My Father," *New York Times*, 27 January 2008.

58. Mike Allen and Carrie Budoff Brown, "Kennedy Kin Back Obama," *Politico*,

28 January 2008; Chris Cillizza, "How Ted Kennedy Helped Change the Course of the 2008 Election," *Washington Post*, 30 March 2015.

59. Jennifer Parker, "Clinton's Delegate Math Challenge," 13 February 2008, www.abcnews.go.com; Ben Smith, "Plouffe: She Can't Catch Us," *Politico*, 13 February 2008.

60. Marc Ambinder, "Clinton's Closing Argument to Superdelegates," *Atlantic*, 28 May 2008; John Harwood, "Democratic Primary Fight Is Like No Other, Ever," *New York Times*, 2 June 2008.

61. Ben Smith, "Obama Locks in Democratic Nomination," *Politico*, 3 June 2008; Adam Nagourney and Jeff Zeleny, "Clinton to End Bid and Endorse Obama," *New York Times*, 5 June 2008. Among the many excellent narratives about the fierce competition for the Democratic presidential nomination, two particularly compelling and instructive sources are David Plouffe, *The Audacity to Win: The Inside Story and Lessons of Barack Obama's Historic Victory* (New York: Viking, 2009), and John Heilemann and Mark Halperin, *Game Change: Obama and the Clintons, McCain and Palin, and the Race of a Lifetime* (New York: HarperCollins, 2010).

62. Adam Nagourney, "Chance of an Obama-Clinton Ticket Is Seen as Increasingly Unlikely," *New York Times*, 29 July 2008; Mark Mooney, "Bill Clinton Pushes Hillary for Vice President," 23 May 2008, www.abcnews.go.com.

63. "Transcript: Hillary Clinton's Prime-Time Speech," National Public Radio, 26 May 2008, www.npr.org.

64. "Transcript: Barack Obama's Acceptance Speech," National Public Radio, 28 August 2008, www.npr.org.

65. "Election 2008: The Third Presidential Debate," *New York Times*, 15 October 2008.

66. Adam Nagourney, "Obama Wins Election," *New York Times*, 4 November 2008.

67. Tom Rosentiel, "Inside Obama's Sweeping Victory," Pew Research Center, 5 November 2008; Michael Nelson, "Barack Obama: Campaigns and Elections," Miller Center, University of Virginia, https://millercenter.org/president/obama/campaigns-and-elections.

68. Senate Democrats gained a filibuster-proof majority of sixty seats after Arlen Specter (R-PA) switched to the Democratic Party in April 2009 and comedian Al Franken (D-MN) prevailed in a recount in June. See "Election Results 2008," *New York Times*, 9 December 2008; Carl Hulse and Adam Nagourney, "Specter Switches Parties; More Heft for Democrats," *New York Times*, 28 April 2009; Emily Pierce, "Franken's Victory Gets Democrats to 60, Sort Of," *Roll Call*, 30 June 2009.

69. "Transcript of Barack Obama's Victory Speech," National Public Radio, 5 November 2008.

70. Alexander Burns, "Obama Announces Transition-Team Staff," *Politico*, 6 November 2008.

71. Peter Baker and Helene Cooper, "Clinton Is Said to Accept Secretary of

State Position," *New York Times*, 21 November 2008; David Morgan, "Gates to Stay as U.S. Defense Secretary: Report," Reuters, 25 November 2008.

72. Jeff Zeleny, "Daschle Ends Bid for Post; Obama Concedes Mistake," *New York Times*, 3 February 2009; White House Office of the Press Secretary, "President Obama Nominates Governor Kathleen Sebelius Secretary of HHS, Announces Release of $155 Million of ARRA Funds for Health Clinics across America," 2 March 2009, https://obamawhitehouse.archives.gov/the-press-office/president-obama-nominates-governor-kathleen-sebelius-secretary-hhs-announces-releas.

73. Barack Obama, "Press Release: Additions to Legislative Affairs Team," Gerhard Peters and John T. Woolley, American Presidency Project, https://www.presidency.ucsb.edu/node/285824; Anna Palmer, "Legislative Affairs Team Gets to Work," *Roll Call*, 20 January 2009.

74. Rosenstiel, "Inside Obama's Sweeping Victory."

CHAPTER 3. OBAMA'S EARLY PRESIDENTIAL LEADERSHIP AND POLICYMAKING EFFORTS

1. Brasfield, *Affordable Care Act*, 60; Jacob Hacker, "The Road to Somewhere: Why Health Reform Happened: Or, Why Political Scientists Who Write about Public Policy Shouldn't Assume They Know How Shape It," *Perspectives on Politics* 8, 3 (September 2010): 861–876.

2. Glenn Thrush and Carrie Budoff Brown, "Obama's Health Care Conversion," *Politico*, 22 September 2013. Also see Jack B. Greenberg, "Why Health Care Came First, and Other Observations on Barack Obama's Early Domestic Policy Agenda," in *Evaluating the Obama Presidency: From Transformational Goals to Governing Realities*, ed. Meena Bose and Paul Fritz (New York: De Gruyter, 2024).

3. Robert Pear and Sheryl Gay Stolberg, "Obama Says He Is Open to Altering Health Plan," *New York Times*, 5 March 2009.

4. Lawrence R. Jacobs and Theda Skocpol, *Health Care Reform and American Politics: What Everyone Needs to Know*, rev. and exp. ed. (New York: Oxford University Press, 2012), 46.

5. "Remarks of President Barack Obama—As Prepared for Delivery, Address to Joint Session of Congress," 24 February 2009, Obama White House online archives.

6. "Obama Begins Health Reform Drive with W. House Forum," Reuters, 5 March 2009; "Obama's Deal: Chronology," *Frontline*, https://www.pbs.org/wgbh/pages/frontline/obamasdeal/etc/cron.html.

7. Cammie Croft, "White House Forum on Health Reform Report," 30 March 2009, https://obamawhitehouse.archives.gov/blog/2009/03/30/white-house-forum-health-reform-report; "Obama Holds Health Summit at White House," *PBS NewsHour*, 5 March 2009, https://www.pbs.org/newshour/health/health-jan-june09-healthcare_03-05.

8. Timothy S. Jost, "Health Care Reform and a Failed Vision of Bipartisanship," *Health Affairs* 35, 10 (October 2016), https://www.healthaffairs.org/doi/10.1377/hlthaff.2016.1080.

9. Norm Ornstein, "The Real Story of Obamacare's Birth," *Atlantic*, 6 July 2015.

10. Richard Knox, "Romney's Mission: Massachusetts Health Care," National Public Radio: Weekend Edition, 8 April 2006; David Welna, "Romney as Governor: 800 Vetoes and One Big Deal," *All Things Considered*, National Public Radio, 13 June 2012.

11. Brasfield, *Affordable Care Act*, 36–37.

12. "Obama Touts Single-Payer System for Health Care," *Wall Street Journal*, 19 August 2008.

13. Elizabeth Popp Berman, *Thinking Like an Economist: How Efficiency Replaced Equality in Public Policy* (Princeton, NJ: Princeton University Press, 2022).

14. Brasfield, *Affordable Care Act*, 40.

15. Byron W. Marshall and Bruce C. Wolpe, *The Committee: A Study of Policy, Power, Politics, and Obama's Historic Legislative Agenda on Capitol Hill* (Ann Arbor: University of Michigan Press, 2018), 52.

16. Jost, "Health Care Reform."

17. Senate Finance Committee chairman Max Baucus (D-MT), "Call to Action: Health Reform 2009," 12 November 2008, https://www.finance.senate.gov/imo/media/doc/finalwhitepaper1.pdf.

18. Jost, "Health Care Reform."

19. Ornstein, "Real Story of Obamacare's Birth."

20. Marshall and Wolpe, *Committee*, 53. Also see Matthew N. Green, *Underdog Politics: The Minority Party in the U.S. House of Representatives* (New Haven, CT: Yale University Press, 2015); Frances E. Lee, *Insecure Majorities: Congress and the Perpetual Campaign* (Chicago: University of Chicago Press, 2016); Barbara Sinclair, *Legislators, Leaders, and Lawmaking: The U.S. House of Representatives in the Postreform Era* (Baltimore: Johns Hopkins University Press, 1995).

21. Ornstein, "Real Story of Obamacare's Birth"; Marshall and Wolpe, *Committee*, 53.

22. Marshall and Wolpe, *Committee*, 53. Also see Richard Fleisher and Jon R. Bond, "The Shrinking Middle in Congress," *British Journal of Political Science* 34 (2004): 429–451; Sean M. Theriault, *Party Polarization in Congress* (New York: Cambridge University Press, 2008).

23. Barack Obama, *A Promised Land* (New York: Crown, 2020), 391.

24. Obama, 381–382.

25. Obama, 381–382.

26. Matt Bai, "Taking the Hill," *New York Times Magazine*, 2 June 2009.

27. Kevin Sack, "On Health Care, Obama Tries to Seize the Moment," *New York Times*, 18 June 2009.

28. Shanoor Seervai, "'A Monumental Effort': How Obamacare Was Passed,"

Commonwealth Fund, 20 March 2020; Fatou Ndiaye and Vishal Shankar, "Revolver Spotlight: Elizabeth Fowler," Revolving Door Project, 28 July 2021.

29. Stuart Altman and David Schactman, *Power, Politics, and Universal Health Care: The Inside Story of a Century-Long Battle* (New York: Prometheus Books, 2011), 332.

30. Steven Brill, *America's Bitter Pill* (New York: Random House, 2015), 91.

31. Sack, "On Health Care."

32. "Obama's Deal."

33. "Obama's Deal."

34. "Obama to Single Payer Advocates: Drop Dead," Physicians for a National Health Program, 3 March 2009, https://www.pnhp.org/news/2009/march/obama_to_single_paye.php.

35. Ben Smith, "Obama Rejects Single Payer," *Politico*, 15 June 2009.

36. Smith.

37. Robert Pear, "House Committee Approves Health Care Bill," *New York Times*, 16 July 2009.

38. Mike Allen, "Doctors Back House Health Bill," *Politico*, 16 July 2009.

39. Associated Press, "Health Bill May Not Curb Health Care Costs," 16 July 2009, www.cbsnews.com.

40. Robert Pear and David M. Herszenhorn, "Democrats Grow Wary as Health Bill Advances," *New York Times*, 17 July 2009.

41. Patrick O'Connor, "Obama Health Plan Passes Key Hurdle," *Politico*, 31 July 2009; Robert Pear and David M. Herszenhorn, "Health Bill Clears Hurdle and Hints at Consensus," *New York Times*, 31 July 2009.

42. Emily Smith, "Timeline of the Health Care Law," 28 June 2012, www.cnnpolitics.com.

43. "Obama's Deal."

44. Reuters, "Drug Makers Agree to Offer Medicare Discounts," *New York Times*, 20 June 2009; US Senate Committee on Finance, "Baucus, Pharmaceutical Companies Announce Deal to Reduce Prescription Drug Costs for Seniors," 20 June 2009; *Washington Post* staff, *Landmark: The Inside Story of America's New Health-Care Law and What It Means for Us All* (New York: Public Affairs, 2010), 18–24.

45. Tom Hamburger, "Discord over White House Drug Accord," *Los Angeles Times*, 14 August 2009; Rich Lowry, "National Review Online: Obama's Backroom Drug Deal," 11 August 2009, www.npr.org.

46. Pear and Herszenhorn, "Democrats Grow Wary."

47. Pear and Herszenhorn.

48. Obama, *Promised Land*, 399.

49. Obama, 401–407.

50. Lawrence Rosenthal and Christine Trost, *Steep: The Precipitous Rise of the Tea Party* (Berkeley: University of California Press, 2012); Alan I. Abramowitz, "Partisan Polarization and the Rise of the Tea Party Movement" (paper presented at the annual meeting of the American Political Science Association, Seattle, 1–4 September 2011).

51. Matthew Bigg and Nick Carey, "Protestors Disrupt Town-Hall Healthcare Talks," 7 August 2009, http://reuters.com.
52. Don Gonyea, "From the Start, Obama Struggled with Fallout from a Kind of Fake News," 10 January 2017, http://npr.org.
53. Gonyea; John Whitesides, "U.S. Healthcare Town Halls: Anger, Fear and Lunacy," 12 August 2009, http://reuters.com.
54. Richard Benedetto, "Summer Ends, Obama's Approval Dips," *Politico*, 1 September 2009.
55. Edward M. Kennedy Institute for the US Senate, "Senator Edward M. Kennedy: 1932–2009—The Life of Ted Kennedy," http://www.tedkennedy.org/biography.html. Also see Ron Elving and Brian Naylor, "Ted Kennedy, Senate's Liberal Lion, Dies," 26 August 2009, http://npr.org.
56. Obama, *Promised Land*, 374–375.
57. George W. Bush, "Address to a Joint Session of Congress and the American People," 20 September 2001, https://georgewbush-whitehouse.archives.gov/news/releases/2001/09/20010920-8.html; Bill Clinton, "Address on Health Care Reform," 22 September 1993.
58. Obama, *Promised Land*, 410.
59. "Obama's Health Care Speech to Congress," *New York Times*, 9 September 2009.
60. "Kennedy's Letter to Obama," *New York Times*, 9 September 2009; Marshall and Wolpe, *Committee*, 72–73.
61. Mashall and Wolpe, *Committee*, 72–73; Brill, *America's Bitter Pill*, 161.
62. Robert Pear, "Public Option Fades from Debate over Health Care," *New York Times*, 12 September 2009.
63. Pear.
64. Hacker, "Road to Somewhere," 868.
65. Altman and Schactman, *Power, Politics, and Universal Health Care*, 286.
66. Pear, "Public Option Fades."
67. Maggie Astor, "What Is the Hyde Amendment? A Look at Its Impact as Biden Reverses His Stance," *New York Times*, 7 June 2019.
68. Jonathan Allen, "Abortion Deal Spins a Very Tangled Web," *Politico*, 16 November 2009.
69. David M. Herszenhorn and Jackie Calmes, "Abortion Was at Heart of Wrangling," *New York Times*, 7 November 2009; Alex Wayne, "House Passes Health Care Overhaul Bill," Commonwealth Fund, 7 November 2009.
70. "House Passes Health Care Reform Bill," CNN, 8 November 2009.
71. Carl Hulse and Robert Pear, "Sweeping Health Care Plan Passes House," *New York Times*, 7 November 2009.
72. "House Passes Health Care Reform Bill"; Patrick O'Connor, "House Passes Historic Health Bill," *Politico*, 7 November 2009.
73. Robert Pear and David M. Herszenhorn, "G.O.P. Counters with a Health Plan of Its Own," *New York Times*, 3 November 2009.
74. Hulse and Pear, "Sweeping Health Care Plan Passes House."

75. "House Passes Health Care Reform Bill"; Marshall and Wolpe, *Committee*, 83.
76. Quoted in Robert Pear and Sheryl Gay Stolberg, "Obama Strategy on Health Legislation Appears to Pay Off," *New York Times*, 1 November 2009.
77. Robert Pear and David M. Herszenhorn, "Health Care Vote Illustrates Partisan Divide," *New York Times*, 15 July 2009; David M. Herszenhorn and Robert Pear, "Health Policy Is Carved out at Table for 6," *New York Times*, 27 July 2009.
78. Ted Barnett, "Senators: No Health Care Deal until Recess Is Over," 29 July 2009, http://cnn.com.
79. John Harwood, "Stronger Prospects for the President on a Health Care Bill," *New York Times*, 30 August 2009.
80. Obama, *Promised Land*, 408.
81. Liz Halloran, "Is Grassley Abandoning Bipartisan Health Bill?" National Public Radio, 20 August 2009.
82. Harwood, "Stronger Prospects for the President."
83. Obama, *Promised Land*, 413.
84. *Washington Post* staff, *Landmark*, 43.
85. *Washington Post* staff, 39–47.
86. Obama, *Promised Land*, 413–415.
87. Chris Frates, "Payoffs for States Get Reid to 60," *Politico*, 19 December 2009; David M. Herszenhorn and Carl Hulse, "Democrats Clinch Deal for Deciding Vote on Health Care Bill," *New York Times*, 19 December 2009.
88. John Whitesides, "Senate on Track to Pass Healthcare Bill," Reuters, 20 December 2009.
89. Alan Silverleib, "Senate Approves Health Care Reform Bill," 24 December 2009, http://cnn.com.
90. Silverleib.
91. In the summer and fall of 2009 several reporters discussed the importance of the public option for many Democrats. See, for example, Jeff Mason, "Obama Stands by Public Option in Healthcare Debate," Reuters, 20 August 2009.
92. Hulse and Pear, "Sweeping Health Care Plan Passes House."
93. O'Connor, "House Passes Historic Health Bill."
94. Robert Pear, "Senate Passes Health Care Overhaul on Party-Line Vote," *New York Times*, 24 December 2009.

CHAPTER 4. OBAMA SUCCEEDS IN ENACTING THE AFFORDABLE CARE ACT

1. "Kennedy's Letter to Obama," *New York Times*, 9 September 2009.
2. Michael Falcone, "Mass. Considers Kennedy's Plan," *Politico*, 28 August 2009.
3. Ross Kerber, "Massachusetts Governor Backs Naming Kennedy Successor," Reuters, 31 August 2009; Abby Goodnough and Carl Hulse, "Former Kennedy Aide Is Appointed to Fill His Senate Seat," *New York Times*, 24 September 2009; "Paul Kirk to Fill Kennedy's Senate Seat," 24 September 2009, www.cnn.com.
4. David Herszenhorn and Robert Pear, "Health Bill Passes Key Test in the

Senate," *New York Times*, 21 December 2009; "Senate Passes $871 Billion Health Care Reform Bill," 24 December 2009, www.money.cnn.com; Bob Oakes, "Interim Senator Kirk Makes Health Vote in Kennedy's Stead," 25 December 2009, www.wbur.org.

5. Frank James, "Mass. AG Martha Coakley Announces Bid for Kennedy's Senate Seat," National Public Radio, 3 September 2009; Alex Isenstadt, "Bay State Women Propel Coakley," *Politico*, 10 September 2009.

6. Joe Duburro, "Former U.S. Rep. Joseph Kennedy Nixes Senate Campaign to Run for Uncle Ted Kennedy's Seat," 7 September 2009, www.masslive.com.

7. Scott Malone, "Coakley Wins Mass. Primary for Kennedy's Senate Seat," Reuters, 8 December 2009; Abby Goodnough, "Top Lawyer Wins Primary to Replace Kennedy," *New York Times*, 8 December 2009.

8. Katie Zezima, "Recognition Woes Hinder G.O.P. Legislator's Run," *New York Times*, 9 December 2009.

9. Zezima.

10. Adam Sorensen, "The Top 10 Everything of 2010: Top Ten Political Gaffes—7. Martha Coakley's Unforced Error," *Time*, 9 December 2010.

11. US Senate special election, Massachusetts, 2010, www.ballotpedia.org; "Republican Scott Brown Defeats Democrat Martha Coakley in Mass. Senate Race," 19 January 2010, www.abcnews.go.com.

12. Ken Rudin, "A Watershed Senate Race: How Scott Brown Did It," 20 January 2010, www.npr.org; "Brown Wins Mass. Senate Race in Epic Upset," 18 January 2010, www.nbcnews.com.

13. Quoted in Alexander Burns, "Brown Pulls off Historic Upset," *Politico*, 20 January 2010.

14. Quoted in Burns. Also see Michael Cooper, "GOP Victory Stuns Democrats," *New York Times*, 19 January 2010.

15. Keith Koffler, "Obama Has No Plans to Campaign for Coakley," *Roll Call*, 11 January 2010.

16. Quoted in Frank James, "Obama in Boston Tries to Pull Coakley across Finish Line," National Public Radio, 17 January 2010. Also see Jeff Zeleny, "Democrats Push to Salvage a Flailing Candidacy," *New York Times*, 17 January 2010; Matt Spetalnick, "Obama Scrambles to Save Democratic Senate Seat," Reuters, 17 January 2010.

17. "Brown Stuns Democrats with Project Victory in Mass. Senate Race," *PBS NewsHour*, 19 January 2010; Cooper, "GOP Victory Stuns Democrats."

18. Karen Travers, "Exclusive: President Obama Says Voter Anger, Frustration Key to Republican Victory in Massachusetts Senate," 20 January 2010, www.abcnewsgo.com. Also see Ed Hornick and Kristi Keck, "Democrats Point Fingers after Stunning Loss," 20 January 2010, www.cnn.com; Steven R. Hurst, "Democrats Scramble after Republicans Take Kennedy's Seat," Associated Press, 20 January 2010, www.cp24.com.

19. Liz Halloran, "For Democrats, Mass. Loss Triggers Finger-Pointing," 20 January 2010, www.npr.org.

20. Marshall and Wolpe, *Committee*, 87.
21. Obama, *Promised Land*, 418.
22. Quoted in Peter Baker, "The Limits of Rahmism," *New York Times Magazine*, 8 March 2010.
23. Obama, *Promised Land*, 419–420.
24. Obama, 408–409, 420.
25. White House, "Remarks by the President in State of the Union Address," 27 January 2010, Obama White House online archives.
26. "Transcript: GOP Response to State of the Union Speech," 28 January 2010, www.cnn.com.
27. Dave Cook, "Obama's Spirited Q&A with House Republicans," *Christian Science Monitor*, 29 January 2010.
28. "Obama Has Tense Visit with House Republicans," 1 February 2010, www.npr.org.
29. Patrick O'Connor and Tim Grieve, "Obama Rumbles with House GOP," *Politico*, 29 January 2010.
30. Quoted in *Washington Post* staff, *Landmark*, 53, 54.
31. Jeff Zeleny, "Obama Plans Bipartisan Summit on Health Care," *New York Times*, 7 February 2010.
32. Associated Press, "GOP Cool to Obama's Call for Health Talks," 8 February 2010, www.nbcnews.com. Also see CQ staff, "Obama Challenges Republicans on Health Care Talk," 9 February 2010, www.commonwealthfund.org.
33. Sheryl Gay Stolberg and Robert Pear, "President Urges Focus on Common Ground," *New York Times*, 25 February 2010; "Obama's Deal: Chronology," *Frontline*, https://www.pbs.org/wgbh/pages/frontline/obamasdeal/etc/cron.html.
34. Mariana Alfaro, Grace Panetta, Taylor Ardrey, and Hanna Kang, "How Nancy Pelosi Went from San Francisco Housewife to the Most Powerful Woman in U.S. Politics," *Business Insider*, 15 July 2022; "Nancy Pelosi: How She Rose to the Top—and Stayed There," 2 August 2022, www.bbc.com.
35. Susan Page, excerpt from *Madam Speaker: Nancy Pelosi and the Lessons of Power* (New York: Twelve Press, 2021), published in *Vanity Fair*, 16 April 2021.
36. Molly Ball, excerpt from *Pelosi* (New York: Henry Holt, 2020), published in "How Nancy Pelosi Saved the Affordable Care Act," *Time*, 6 May 2020.
37. Ball.
38. Ball.
39. Richard Kogan and David Reich, "Introduction to Budget 'Reconciliation,'" Center on Budget and Policy Priorities, updated 6 May 2022; David Wessel, "What Is Reconciliation in Congress?" Brookings Institution, 5 February 2021.
40. "Democrats Consider Backup Plan for Health Reform as Mass. Race Remains Tight," 18 January 2010, www.pbs.org.
41. Quoted in Karen Travers and Huma Khan, "President Obama, Democrats: Not Going to Rush Health Care," 21 January 2010, www.abcnews.go.com.
42. Obama, *Promised Land*, 420.

43. Quoted in Sheryl Gay Stolberg and Robert Pear, "Wary Centrists Posing Challenge in Health Care Vote," *New York Times*, 27 February 2010. Also see Edward Epstein, "Pelosi Outlines Health Care Bill, Pushes for Vote," Commonwealth Fund, 12 March 2020. For a comparison of the House and Senate bills, see "Comparing the House and the Senate Health Care Proposals," *New York Times*, 23 February 2009.

44. David M. Herszenhorn and Robert Pear, "Obama Rallies Democrats in Final Push for House Bill," *New York Times*, 20 March 2010; Marshall and Wolpe, *Committee*, 88; Janet Hook and Noam N. Levey, "How Some Democratic Holdouts Made the Call on Healthcare," *Los Angeles Times*, 20 March 2010;

45. Hook and Levey, "How Some Democratic Holdouts Made the Call."

46. Peter Roff, "Pelosi Was against 'Deem and Pass' before She Was for It," *U.S. News & World Report*, 16 March 2010; Catharine Richert, "'Deem and Pass' and What It Really Means," *Tampa Bay Times*, 19 March 2010.

47. Peggy Noonan, "Now for the Slaughter," *Wall Street Journal*, 20 March 2020; Marshall and Wolpe, *Committee*, 89.

48. Herszenhorn and Pear, "Obama Rallies Democrats."

49. Hook and Levey, "How Some Democratic Holdouts Made the Call."

50. Marshall and Wolpe, *Committee*, 89.

51. Alan Fram, "Raucous, Ugly Buildup to House Health Care Vote," *San Diego Union-Tribune*, 20 March 2010.

52. "Obamacare Overview," Ballotpedia.

53. Jonathan Allen, "Only 3 of 45 House Democrats Who Voted 'No' on Obamacare Are Still There," *Vox*, 1 September 2015.

54. Alan Silverleib, "House Passes Health Care Bill on a 219-212 Vote," 22 March 2010, www.cnn.com.

55. Silverleib.

56. "Rep. Dennis Kucinich Switches Health Care Vote," ABC News, 17 March 2010.

57. Critics of Obama's health care plan started calling it "Obamacare" during his first presidential campaign. The Obama White House initially embraced the term, with the president declaring, "We passed Obamacare—yes, I like the term." The administration later decreased its usage during the complicated implementation process. See Reid J. Epstein, "Taking 'Obama' out of Health Care," *Politico*, 19 November 2013.

58. "Remarks by the President and Vice President at Signing of the Health Insurance Reform Bill," 23 March 2010, www.obamawhitehouse.archives.gov.

59. Richard Adams, "Joe Biden: 'This Is a Big F****** Deal!'" *Guardian*, 23 March 2010; Mychael Schnell, "Biden Pokes Fun at 2010 'BFD' Hot Mic Moment during Obama Visit," *Hill*, 5 April 2022.

60. Silverleib, "House Passes Health Care Bill."

61. "Obamacare Overview," Ballotpedia; Congressional Research Service, "Medicare: Changes Made by the Reconciliation Act of 2010 to the Patient Protec-

tion and Affordable Care Act (P.L. 111-148)," 25 March 2010; Alan Frumin, letter to the editor, "Obamacare Was Not Passed Using Budget Reconciliation," *Washington Post*, 22 January 2016.

62. Obama, *Promised Land*, 426.

63. Obama, 425.

CHAPTER 5. OBAMA'S HEALTH CARE REFORM LEGACY: IMPLEMENTING AND UPHOLDING THE ACA

1. National Library of Medicine, "The Impacts of the Affordable Care Act on Preparedness Resources and Programs: Workshop Summary," 27 August 2014, https://www.ncbi.nlm.nih.gov/books/NBK241401/.

2. National Library of Medicine.

3. White House Office of the Press Secretary, "Fact Sheet: The Affordable Care Act: Supporting Innovation, Empowering States," 28 February 2011, https://obamawhitehouse.archives.gov/the-press-office/2011/02/28/fact-sheet-affordable-care-act-supporting-innovation-empowering-states.

4. American Presidency Project, "Seats in Congress Gained/Lost by the President's Party in Mid-term Elections" (Santa Barbara: University of California), https://www.presidency.ucsb.edu/node/332343/.

5. Paul Bedard, "Healthcare Vote Doomed 13 Democrats in 2010 Elections," *U.S. News & World Report*, 12 April 2011; Brendan Nyhan, Eric McGhee, John Sides, Seth Masket, and Steven Greene, "One Vote out of Step? The Effects of Salient Roll Call Votes in the 2010 Election," *American Politics Research* 40, 5 (2012): 844–879.

6. Liz Halloran, "Obama Humbled by Election 'Shellacking,'" National Public Radio, 3 November 2010.

7. Halloran.

8. Obama, *Promised Land*, 594.

9. Warren Richey, "Attorneys General in 14 States Sue to Block Healthcare Reform Law," *Christian Science Monitor*, 23 March 2010.

10. "State Attorneys General against the Patient Protection and Affordable Care Act of 2010," Ballotpedia. The fourteen states that initially filed lawsuits were Alabama, Colorado, Florida, Idaho, Louisiana, Michigan, Nebraska, Pennsylvania, South Carolina, South Dakota, Texas, Utah, Washington (in one case), and Virginia (in a separate lawsuit). Alaska, Arizona, Georgia, Indiana, Iowa, Kansas, Maine, Mississippi, Nevada, North Dakota, Ohio, Wisconsin, and Wyoming later joined in the suits to overturn the ACA.

11. "Obama Warns 'Unelected' Supreme Court Not to Strike Down Health Care Law," *Guardian*, 2 April 2012.

12. Jeff Mason, "Obama Takes a Shot at Supreme Court over Healthcare," Reuters, 2 April 2012.

13. Adam Liptak, "Supreme Court Upholds Health Care Law, 5-4, in Victory for Obama," *New York Times*, 28 June 2012.

14. Chris Cillizza and Aaron Blake, "President Obama Embraces 'Obamacare' Label. But Why?" *Washington Post*, 26 March 2012.
15. Robert J. Blendon, John M. Benson, and Amanda Brule, "Understanding Health Care in the 2012 Election," *New England Journal of Medicine* 367 (2012): 1658–1661.
16. Sara R. Collins, Stuart Guterman, Rachel Nuzum, Mark A. Zezza, Tracy Garber, and Jennie Smith, "Health Care in the 2012 Presidential Election: How the Obama and Romney Plans Stack Up," Commonwealth Fund, 2 October 2012.
17. Ezra Klein and Sarah Kliff, "Obama's Last Campaign: Inside the White House Plan to Sell Obamacare," *Washington Post*, 17 July 2013; Alexander H. Sommer, "State Implementation of the Affordable Care Act," *AMA Journal of Ethics Virtual Mentor* 15 (2013): 603–605.
18. Joseph R. Antos, "Getting Back to Reality: The Election, the Fiscal Cliff, and the ACA," *American Health & Drug Benefits* 5 (November–December 2012): 403–406.
19. "Policy Basics: Introduction to Medicaid," Center on Budget and Policy Priorities, updated 14 April 2020; "Medicaid Eligibility," www.medicaid.gov; "State-Based Exchanges," Centers for Medicare and Medicaid Services.
20. Klein and Kliff, "Obama's Last Campaign."
21. Dan Kedmey, "Ted Cruz Reads 'Green Eggs and Ham' on the Senate Floor—and That's Not the Weird Part," *Time*, 25 September 2013; Philip Bump, Abby Ohlheiser, and Brian Feldman, "Ted Cruz Finishes His Epic Senate Speech after 21 Hours," *Atlantic*, 24 September 2013.
22. John Bresnahan and Jake Sherman, "House Delays Obamacare," *Politico*, 28 September 2013; Jonathan Weisman and Jeremy W. Peters, "Government Shuts down in Budget Impasse," *New York Times*, 30 September 2013.
23. Paige Winfield Cunningham, "Dems OK with Income Verification," *Politico*, 17 October 2013; Kirsten Appleton and Veronica Stracqualursi, "Here's What Happened the Last Time the Government Shut Down," 18 November 2014, www.abcnews.go.com.
24. Robert Pear, Sharon LaFraniere, and Ian Austen, "From the Start, Signs of Trouble at Health Portal," *New York Times*, 12 October 2013.
25. Roberta Rampton, "Days before Launch, Obamacare Website Failed to Handle Even 500 Users," 21 November 2013, www.reuters.com; Tom Cohen, "Rough Obamacare Rollout: 4 Reasons Why," 23 October 2013, www.cnn.com.
26. "Health Insurance Policy Cancellations since Obamacare," Ballotpedia, https://ballotpedia.org/Health_insurance_policy_cancellations_since_Obamacare.
27. Barack Obama, "Speech to the American Medical Association," 15 June 2009, cited in Glenn Kessler, "Obama's Pledge that 'No One Will Take Away' Your Health Plan," *Washington Post*, 30 October 2013.
28. Kessler, "Obama's Pledge."
29. Mark Memmott, "Obama's 'You Can Keep It' Promise Is 'Lie of the Year,'" National Public Radio, 13 December 2013. Also see Lisa Myers and Hannah Rappleye, "Obama Admin. Knew Millions Could Not Keep Their Health Insurance,"

28 October 2013, www.nbcnews.com; Richard Himelfarb, "'If You Like Your Health Care Plan, You Can Keep Your Health Care Plan': An Analysis of President Barack Obama's Most Infamous Statement" (paper presented at Hofstra University's Thirteenth Presidential Conference, "The Barack Obama Presidency—Hope and Change," 19–21 April 2023).

30. Ashley Parker and Robert Pear, "Obama Moves to Avert Cancellation of Insurance," *New York Times*, 14 November 2013; Lisa Clemans-Cope and Nathaniel Anderson, "How Many Nongroup Policies Were Canceled? Estimates from December 2013," Health Affairs, 3 March 2014, https://www.healthaffairs.org/content/forefront/many-nongroup-policies-were-canceled-estimates-december-2013; Lori Robertson, "'Millions' Lost Insurance," 11 April 2014, www.factcheck.org.

31. Roberta Rampton and Susan Cornwell, "Obama Says 'We Screwed It Up' on Health Law Debut," 20 December 2013, www.reuters.com; Stanley Renshon, "Unfulfilled Hopes: President Obama's Legacy," in *Looking Back on President Barack Obama's Legacy: Hope and Change*, ed. Wilbur C. Rich (New York: Palgrave Macmillan, 2019), 229.

32. Michael D. Shear and Robert Pear, "Obama Admits Web Site Flaws on Health Law," *New York Times*, 21 October 2013.

33. Jason Millman, "Tech 'Surge' to Repair ACA Website," *Politico*, 20 October 2013.

34. Frank James, "White House Turns to 'Rock Star' Manager for Obamacare Fix," 23 October 2013, www.npr.org; Jackie Calmes, "Obama Recalls an Aide to Guide Health Care Law," *New York Times*, 6 December 2013.

35. Phil Schiliro, "The Affordable Care Act Is Working," *Politico*, 24 March 2014; David Nather, "Schiliro's Obamacare Lessons," *Politico*, 23 May 2014.

36. Brendan Mochoruk and Louise Sheiner, "*King v. Burwell* Explained," USC-Brookings Schaefer on Health Policy, 3 March 2015.

37. *King v. Burwell*, Ballotpedia.

38. *King v. Burwell*.

39. Leigh Ann Caldwell, "Obamacare Repeal Fails: Three GOP Senators Rebel in 49–51 Vote," 28 July 2017, www.nbcnews.com; Robert Pear, "Without the Insurance Mandate, Health Care's Future May Be in Doubt," *New York Times*, 18 December 2017; Dylan Scott and Sarah Kliff, "Republicans Have Finally Repealed a Crucial Piece of Obamacare," *Vox*, 20 December 2017.

40. Katie Keith, "State Lawsuit Claims that Individual Mandate Penalty Repeal Should Topple Entire ACA," 28 February 2018, www.healthaffairs.org; Ariane de Vogue and Chandelis Duster, "Supreme Court Dismisses Challenge to Affordable Care Act, Leaving It in Place," 26 June 2021, www.cnn.com.

41. Matt Broaddus and Edwin Park, "Affordable Care Act Has Produced Historic Gains in Health Coverage," Center on Budget and Policy Priorities, 15 December 2016.

42. Steven Rattner, "For Tens of Millions, Obamacare Is Working," *New York Times*, 21 February 2015.

43. Rattner. Also see Miriam Reisman, "The Affordable Care Act, Five Years Later: Policies, Progress, and Politics," *National Library of Medicine PubMed Central* 40, 9 (September 2015): 575–600.

44. Abigail Abrams, "Ten Years Later, Obamacare's Complicated Legacy Still Shapes the Nation," *Time*, 19 March 2020.

45. Abrams.

46. David Blumenthal, Sara R. Collins, and Elizabeth Fowler, "The Affordable Care Act at 10 Years: What's the Effect on Health Care Coverage and Access?" Commonwealth Fund, 26 February 2020.

47. Laxmaiah Manchikanti, Standiford Helm II, Ramsin M. Benyamin, and Joshua A. Hirsch, "A Critical Analysis of Obamacare: Affordable Care or Insurance for Many and Coverage for Few?" *Pain Physician* 20 (March–April 2017): 111–138, www.painphysicianjournal.com.

48. Selena Simmons-Duffin, "12 Holdout States Haven't Expanded Medicaid, Leaving 2 Million People in Limbo," National Public Radio, 1 July 2021; Abby Goodnough, Reed Abelson, Margot Sanger-Katz, and Sarah Kliff, "Obamacare Turns 10: Here's a Look at What Works and What Doesn't," *New York Times*, 8 March 2021.

49. Sarah O'Brien, "Expanded Health Insurance Subsidies Remain Intact for 13 Million People under Inflation Reduction Act," 8 August 2022, https://www.cnbc.com/2022/08/08/expanded-health-care-subsidies-stay-intact-under-inflation-reduction-act.html. Also see Sabrina Corlette, Linda J. Blumberg, and Kevin Lucia, "The ACA's Effect on the Individual Insurance Market," *Health Affairs* 39, 3 (March 2020): 436–444.

50. David M. Herszenhorn, "A Grand Achievement, or a Lost Opportunity?" *New York Times*, 24 March 2010.

51. Tami Luhby, "Health Care Explained: Medicare for All vs Public Option vs the ACA," 30 July 2019, https://www.cnn.com/2019/07/30/politics/health-care-explainer/index.html.

52. An instructive study that refutes congressional critiques of the ACA during the policymaking process in 2009–10 with a data analysis ten years after the law's full implementation is Co-Equal, "The Affordable Care Act: Comparing Congressional Rhetoric with Reality," March 2024.

CONCLUSION: ASSESSING OBAMA'S LEADERSHIP

1. Dov Weinryb Grohsgal, interview with health policy adviser Jeanne Lambrew, Obama Presidency Oral History, Columbia University, https://obamaoralhistory.columbia.edu/interviews?sort=az&topic=healthcare.

2. Dov Weinryb Grohsgal, interview with White House deputy chief of staff Nancy-Ann DeParle, Obama Presidency Oral History, Columbia University, https://obamaoralhistory.columbia.edu/interviews?topic=healthcare&page=2&sort=az.

3. Dov Weinryb Grohsgal, interview with Secretary of Health and Human

Services Kathleen Sebelius, Obama Presidency Oral History, Columbia University, https://obamaoralhistory.columbia.edu/interviews?topic=healthcare&page=2&sort=az.

4. Dov Weinryb Grohsgal, interview with health policy official Elizabeth Fowler, Obama Presidency Oral History, Columbia University, https://obamaoralhistory.columbia.edu/interviews?topic=healthcare&page=2&sort=az.

BIBLIOGRAPHIC ESSAY

This appraisal of President Barack Obama's leadership in enacting the Patient Protection and Affordable Care Act of 2010 builds on an extensive scholarship about the Obama presidency, presidential power, and health care policy, as well as scholarly studies of American politics, policymaking, and policy implementation more broadly. This bibliographic essay is by no means exhaustive, but it provides an introduction to the sources that informed this analysis and are instructive for understanding Obama's leadership in enacting the ACA and the law's consequences for American health care. As this book examines a relatively recent event in the Landmark Presidential Decisions series, many news sources were consulted as well and are cited in the endnotes.

Speeches are the main primary sources, and the declassification of documents in the future will produce additional archival sources for research and analysis. In March 2024 the Obama Presidency Oral History at Columbia University published online more than two dozen interviews (out of 450+ in the project) with administration officials, congressional staff, interest-group leaders, and other individuals active in the ACA's enactment and implementation. A few of these interviews are cited in this study, which was published shortly thereafter. Over time, these and other primary sources will enrich the narrative of Obama's leadership related to the ACA.

Other useful primary sources for understanding the perspectives on leadership and policymaking in the Obama administration are participants' memoirs. President Obama's *A Promised Land* (New York: Crown, 2020) is a lengthy and insightful exploration of his election and first two and a half years in office, with ample attention to health care reform and passage of the ACA. Michelle Obama's *Becoming* (New York: Crown, 2018) is an engaging behind-the-scenes narrative of highlights and challenges for President Obama, the First Lady, and their family. Memoirs that provide context for Obama's early policy priorities and challenges, with important implications for the ACA's passage and implementation, include David Axelrod, *Believer: My Forty Years in Politics* (New York: Penguin Books, 2016); Timothy F. Geithner, *Stress Test:*

Reflections on Financial Crises (New York: Crown, 2014); Valerie Jarrett, *Finding My Voice: My Journey to the West Wing and the Path Forward* (New York: Viking, 2019; reprint, Penguin Books, 2020); and David Plouffe, *The Audacity to Win: How Obama Won and How We Can Beat the Party of Limbaugh, Beck and Palin* (New York: Penguin Books, 2010).

A special conference hosted by the University of Virginia in March 2024 addressed significant topics related to the ACA's passage and implementation, and a publication summarizing key findings is forthcoming. Additionally, the nonprofit organization Co-Equal, which Obama adviser Philip M. Schiliro helped create, published "The Affordable Care Act: Comparing Congressional Rhetoric with Reality" on the organization's website in 2024 to refute critics who predicted multiple problems with the law.

Several of Obama's foreign policy and national security advisers have written memoirs that are instructive for understanding the early Obama presidency, including Hillary Rodham Clinton, *Hard Choices* (New York: Simon & Schuster, 2014); Robert M. Gates, *Duty: Memoirs of a Secretary at War* (New York: Vintage, 2015); Leon Panetta, *Worthy Fights: A Memoir of Leadership in War and Peace* (New York: Penguin Books, 2014); Samantha Power, *The Education of an Idealist* (New York: Dey Street Books, 2019); Ben Rhodes, *The World as It Is: A Memoir of the Obama White House* (New York: Random House, 2018; paperback ed., 2019); and Susan Rice, *Tough Love: My Story of the Things Worth Fighting For* (New York: Simon & Schuster, 2019).

Informative books by journalists about Obama's life, political career, and presidency include the following: Jonathan Alter, *The Promise: President Obama, Year One* (New York: Simon & Schuster, 2010); Christopher Andersen, *Barack and Michelle: Portrait of an American Marriage* (New York: William Morrow, 2009); David Garrow, *Rising Star: The Making of Barack Obama* (New York: William Morrow, 2017); David Maraniss, *Barack Obama: The Story* (New York: Simon & Schuster, 2013); David Mendell, *Obama: From Promise to Power* (New York: Amistad, 2007); David Remnick, *The Bridge: The Life and Rise of Barack Obama* (New York: Knopf, 2010); Janny Scott, *A Singular Woman: The Untold Story of Barack Obama's Mother* (New York: Riverhead Books, 2011); Jeffrey Toobin, *The Oath: The Obama White House and the Supreme Court* (New

York: Doubleday, 2012); and Richard Wolffe, *Renegade: The Making of a President* (New York: Crown, 2009).

For scholarly studies of the Obama presidency that evaluate his leadership, achievements, challenges, and legacy, representative sources include Meena Bose and Paul Fritz, eds., *Evaluating the Obama Presidency: From Transformational Goals to Governing Realities* (New York: De Gruyter Academic Publishing, forthcoming); Claude A. Clegg III, *The Black President: Hope and Fury in the Age of Obama* (Baltimore: Johns Hopkins University Press, 2021); George C. Edwards III, *Overreach: Leadership in the Obama Presidency* (Princeton, NJ: Princeton University Press, 2012); George C. Edwards III, *Predicting the Presidency: The Potential of Persuasive Leadership* (Princeton, NJ: Princeton University Press, 2016); Andra Gillespie, *Race and the Obama Administration: Substance, Symbols, and Hope* (Manchester, UK: Manchester University Press, 2019); Martha Joynt Kumar, *Before the Oath: How George W. Bush and Barack Obama Managed a Transfer of Power* (Baltimore: Johns Hopkins University Press, 2015); Manning Marable and Kristen Clarke, eds., *Barack Obama and African American Empowerment: The Rise of Black America's New Leadership* (New York: Palgrave Macmillan, 2009); James P. Pfiffner, "Decision Making in the Obama White House," *Presidential Studies Quarterly* 41, 2 (June 2011): 244–262; Wilbur C. Rich, ed., *Looking Back on Barack Obama's Legacy: Hope and Change* (New York: Palgrave Macmillan, 2019); Steven E. Schier, ed., *Debating the Obama Presidency* (New York: Rowman & Littlefield, 2016); and John Kenneth White, *Barack Obama's America: How New Conceptions of Race, Family, and Religion Ended the Reagan Era* (Ann Arbor: University of Michigan Press, 2009).

Selected analyses of US health care policy and the Affordable Care Act include the following: Stuart Altman and David Schactman, *Power, Politics, and Universal Health Care: The Inside Story of a Century-Long Battle* (New York: Prometheus Books 2011); Ann-Laure Beaussier, "The Patient Protection and Affordable Care Act: The Victory of Unorthodox Lawmaking," *Journal of Health Politics, Policy and Law* 37, 5 (2012): 741–778; Daniel Beland, Philip Rocco, and Alex Waddan, *Obamacare Wars: Federalism, State Politics, and the Affordable Care Act* (Lawrence: University Press of Kansas, 2016); David Blumenthal and James Monroe, *The Heart of Power with a New Preface: Health and Politics in the Oval Office* (Berkeley: University of California Press, 2010); David W. Brady and Daniel P. Kessler, "Why Is Health Reform so Difficult?" *Journal of Health Politics, Policy and Law* 35, 2 (April 2010): 161–175; James M. Brasfield, *The Affordable Care Act: At the Nexus of Politics and Policy* (Boulder, CO: Lynne Rienner, 2022); Steven Brill, *America's Bitter Pill* (New York: Random House, 2015); Jacob Hacker, "The Road to Somewhere: Why Health Reform Happened: Or, Why Political Scientists Who Write about Public Policy Shouldn't Assume They Know How to Shape It," *Perspectives on Politics* 8, 3 (September 2010): 861–876; Beatrix Hoffman, "Health Care Reform and Social Movements in the United States," *American Journal of Public Health* 93, 1 (January 2003): 75–85; Lawrence R. Jacobs and Theda Skocpol, *Health Care Reform and American Politics: What Everyone Needs to Know*, rev. and exp. ed. (New York: Oxford University Press, 2012); Timothy S. Jost, "Health Care Reform and a Failed Vision of Bipartisanship," *Health Affairs* 35, 10 (October 2016): 1748–1752; Jonathan Oberlander, "Lessons from the Long and Winding Road to Medicare for All," *American Journal of Public Health* 109, 11 (2019): 1497–1500; Monte Poen, *Harry S. Truman versus the Medical Lobby: The Genesis of Medicare* (Columbia: University of Missouri Press, 1979); Paul Starr, *Remedy and Reaction: The Peculiar American Struggle over Health Care Reform* (New Haven, CT: Yale University Press, 2011); Paul Starr, *The Social Transformation of American Medicine* (New York: Basic Books, 1982); and *Washington Post* staff, *Landmark: The Inside Story of America's New Health-Care Law and What It Means for Us All* (New York: Public Affairs, 2010).

Many studies of modern presidential leadership, from agenda setting to power politics to policymaking, informed this analysis. See, for example, Meena Bose and Mark Landis, eds., *The Uses and Abuses of Presidential Ratings* (Hauppauge, NY: Nova Science Publishers, 2003); John P. Burke, *The Institutional Presidency* (Baltimore: Johns Hopkins University Press, 1992); John P. Burke, *Presidential Power: Theories and Dilemmas* (New York: Routledge, 2019); John P. Burke and Fred I. Greenstein, with Larry Berman and Richard Immerman, *How Presidents Test Reality: Decisions on Vietnam, 1954 and 1965* (New York: Russell Sage Foundation, 1989); James MacGregor Burns, *Leadership* (New York: HarperCollins,

1978); Edward S. Corwin, *The President: Office and Powers* (New York: NYU/George Grady Press, 1940); Thomas E. Cronin, Michael A. Genovese, and Meena Bose, *The Paradoxes of the American Presidency*, 6th ed. (New York: Oxford University Press, 2022); George C. Edwards III, *At the Margins: Presidential Leadership of Congress* (New Haven, CT: Yale University Press, 1990); George C. Edwards III, Kenneth R. Mayer, and Stephen J. Wayne, *Presidential Leadership: Politics and Policy Making*, 12th ed. (New York: Rowman & Littlefield, 2022); Jeff Fishel, *Presidents and Promises: From Campaign Pledge to Presidential Performance* (Washington, DC: CQ Press, 1985); Matthew N. Green, *Underdog Politics: The Minority Party in the U.S. House of Representatives* (New Haven, CT: Yale University Press, 2015); Fred I. Greenstein, "Can Personality and Politics Be Studied Systematically?" *Political Psychology* 13, 1 (March 1992): 105–128; Fred I. Greenstein, *The Presidential Difference: Leadership Style from FDR to Barack Obama*, 3rd ed. (Princeton, NJ: Princeton University Press, 2009); Stephen Hess and James P. Pfiffner, *Organizing the Presidency*, 3rd ed. (Washington, DC: Brookings Institution Press, 2002); Samuel Kernell, *Going Public: New Strategies of Presidential Leadership*, 4th ed. (Washington, DC: CQ Press, 2006); John W. Kingdon, *Agendas, Alternatives, and Public Policies*, updated 2nd ed., with epilogue on health care reform (New York: Longman, 2011); Frances E. Lee, *Insecure Majorities: Congress and the Perpetual Campaign* (Chicago: University of Chicago Press, 2016); Sidney M. Milkis and Michael Nelson, *The American Presidency: Origins and Development, 1776–2021*, 9th ed. (Washington, DC: CQ Press, 2023); Richard E. Neustadt, *Presidential Power and the Modern Presidents* (New York: Free Press, 1990); James P. Pfiffner, *The Strategic Presidency: Hitting the Ground Running*, 2nd rev. ed. (Lawrence: University Press of Kansas, 1996); Daniel Ponder, *Good Advice: Information and Policy Making in the White House* (College Station: Texas A&M University Press, 2000); Andrew Rudalevige, *Managing the President's Program: Presidential Leadership and Legislative Policy Formulation* (Princeton, NJ: Princeton University Press, 2002); Barbara Sinclair, *Legislators, Leaders, and Lawmaking: The U.S. House of Representatives in the Postreform Era* (Baltimore: Johns Hopkins University Press, 1995); Charles E. Walcott and Karen M. Hult, *Governing the White House: From Hoover through LBJ* (Lawrence: University Press of Kansas, 1995); and Thomas J. Weko, *The*

Politicizing Presidency: The White House Personnel Office, 1948–1994 (Lawrence: University Press of Kansas, 1995).

Additionally, studies of US policymaking, polarization in American politics, and policy implementation contributed to this analysis. Sample texts include Alan I. Abramowitz, *The Great Alignment: Race, Party Transformation, and the Rise of Donald Trump* (New Haven, CT: Yale University Press, 2018); Elizabeth Popp Berman, *Thinking Like an Economist: How Efficiency Replaced Equality in Public Policy* (Princeton, NJ: Princeton University Press, 2022); Morris P. Fiorina, *Unstable Majorities: Polarization, Party Sorting, and Political Stalemate* (Stanford, CA: Hoover Institution Press, 2017); Richard Fleisher and Jon R. Bond, "The Shrinking Middle in Congress," *British Journal of Political Science* 34 (2004): 429–451; Daniel Galvin and Colleen Shogan, "Presidential Politicization and Centralization across the Modern-Traditional Divide," *Polity* 36, 3 (April 2004): 477–504; Ezra Klein, *Why We're Polarized* (New York: Simon & Schuster, 2020); Lilliana Mason, *Uncivil Agreement: How Politics Became Our Identity* (Chicago: University of Chicago Press, 2018); Lawrence Rosenthal and Christine Trost, *Steep: The Precipitous Rise of the Tea Party* (Berkeley: University of California Press, 2012); Brandon Rottinghaus, Gregory Eady, and Justin S. Vaughn, "Presidential Greatness in a Polarized Era: Results from the Latest Presidential Greatness Survey," *PS: Political Science & Politics* 53, 3 (2020): 413–420; Brandon Rottinghaus and Justin S. Vaughn, "Official Results of the 2024 Presidential Greatness Project Expert Survey," 19 February 2024, http://www.brandonrottinghaus.com/uploads/1/0/8/7/108798321/presidential_greatness_white_paper_2024.pdf; and Sean M. Theriault, *Party Polarization in Congress* (New York: Cambridge University Press, 2008).

INDEX

abortion, 59, 76, 79
Affordable Care Act (ACA) (Patient Protection and Affordable Care Act)
   ambivalence regarding, 7
   challenges of, 82, 85–89, 92
   changes to, 97
   constitutionality of, 82
   enactment of, 74–79
   flexibility regarding, 83, 86–89, 97
   goals of, 91–92
   grandfathering into, 88
   initial effects of, 82–84
   as Obamacare, 78, 86, 117n57
   passage of, 78
   polarization regarding, 2
   in practice, 85–86
   promises regarding, 53
   provisions of, 78–79, 88
   public opinion regarding, 7
   repeal of, 90
   signing of, 2
   statistics regarding, 91
Affordable Health Care for America Act, 59, 61, 62, 63
African Americans, 32, 91
Alabama, lawsuit of, 118n10
Alaska, lawsuit of, 118n10
Alito, Samuel, 85
American Association for Labor Legislation, 13
American Federation of Labor (AFL), 13
American Medical Association (AMA), 13–14, 15, 52, 54, 62
American Public Health Association, 12–13
American Rescue Plan, 92
America's Affordable Health Choices Act, 54
Arizona, lawsuit of, 118n10
Axelrod, David, 35, 67, 70, 71–72

Bader Ginsburg, Ruth, 85. *See* Ginsburg, Ruth Bader

Baucus, Max, 49–50, 55–56, 60–61
Biden, Joe, 42, 52, 78
Bingaman, Jeff, 50
Blair House, 72
Boehner, John, 71
Breyer, Stephen, 85
Brown, Scott, 67
budget and reconciliation process, 74–79, 96–97
Bunning, Jim, 62
Burns, James MacGregor, 8
Bush, George H. W., 19
Bush, George W., 5–6, 43, 57

Cadillac health plans, 63
Cao, Anh, 59
Cardoza, Dennis, 76
Carville, James, 20
Children's Health Insurance Program, 89
Clinton, Hillary Rodham
   challenges of, 24
   criticism of, 23
   election statistics of, 40–41
   endorsement by, 42
   leadership of, 19, 20
   leadership style of, 23
   presidential candidacy of, 37, 39–40
   supporters of, 42
   testimony of, 22
Clinton, William "Bill" Jefferson
   campaign promises of, 20
   economic focus of, 20
   governing challenges of, 19, 21–22, 23, 24
   on health care, 11, 22
   health care work of, 2, 9, 19–24
   on Hillary's leadership, 24
   policy announcement of, 57
   reelection of, 24
Coakley, Martha, 66–68
Cold War, 15
Colorado, lawsuit of, 118n10
Committee on the Costs of Medical Care, 13–14

Commonwealth Fund report, 91–92
Congress
  bipartisan summit in, 72
  budgetary process of reconciliation and, 74–79, 96–97
  budget legislation by, 87
  filibuster-proof majority loss in, 10, 65–69, 96, 109n68
  health care legislation model of, 48, 51–57, 95
  See also House of Representatives; Senate
Congressional Budget Act, 74–79
Congressional Budget Office (CBO), 54
Connolly, Ceci, 53
Conrad, Kent, 50, 58
Cornyn, John, 67
Corwin, Edward S., 4
Cruz, Ted, 87

D'Alesandro, Thomas, Jr., 73
Daley, Richard M., 34
Daschle, Tom, 44, 52
Dean, Howard, 61
Democratic National Convention, 35, 36
Democratic Party
  bipartisan discussions of, 50–51
  Blue Dog, 58
  concerns of, 76–77
  dissension within, 71–72
  election results of, 23, 83
  health care reform discussion by, 58–59, 60, 63
  health care work of, 13
  losing filibuster-proof majority by, 10, 65–69, 96, 109n68
  Medicare opposition by, 18
  nomination by, 39–42
  Obama's session with, 71–72
  public opinion challenges of, 83
  voting statistics of, 59
DeParle, Nancy-Ann, 48, 51, 95
Dreams from My Father (Obama), 30
Drew, Elizabeth, 23
Dunham, Madelyn, 29
Dunham, Stanley, Sr., 29
Dunham, Stanley Ann, 28, 32

Economic Bill of Rights, 14
Education and Labor Committee, 54
Edwards, John, 39
Elmendorf, Doug, 54
Emmanuel, Rahm, 52, 60, 69–70
Energy and Commerce Committee, 54
Enzi, Mike, 50

Federal Advisory Committee Act, 21
Fitzgerald, Peter, 35
Florida, lawsuit of, 118n10
Fowler, Elizabeth, 52, 97
Franken, Al, 109n68

Gang of Six, 50, 55, 60
Gates, Robert, 44
General Motors, 52
Georgia, lawsuit of, 118n10
Gergen, David, 24
Gibbs, Robert, 68
Ginsburg, Ruth Bader, 85
Giuliani, Rudolph W., 39
Grassley, Chuck, 49–50, 55, 56, 60–61
Great Depression, 13
Great Recession, 7
Great Society, 17–18
Greenstein, Fred I., 4
Gregg, Judd, 58

"Harry and Louise" ads, 22–23
Harvard Law Review, 31, 32
Health, Education, Labor, and Pensions (HELP) Committee, 49, 55
healthcare.gov, technical difficulties regarding, 88–89
health care provisions/reform
  advancement of, 69–72
  bill differences regarding, 62–63
  bipartisan coalition for, 50–51, 70–72
  bipartisan discussions regarding, 50–51
  challenges of, 3, 39
  Clinton's work on, 2, 9, 19–24
  components of, 62
  development of, 12
  evolution of, 12–14
  Johnson's work regarding, 2, 9, 11, 16–18

legislative efforts focus for, 57–62, 95–96
legislative plan for, 58
policymaking process for, 48–51, 95
as priority, in 2009, 47, 94
roundtables for, 55
statistics regarding, 91
town hall meetings for, 56
Truman's work regarding, 2, 9, 11, 14–16
White House forum regarding, 48
See also Affordable Care Act (ACA) (Patient Protection and Affordable Care Act)
Health Insurance Association of America (HIAA), 22–23
Hensarling, Jeb, 71
Hispanics, health care coverage of, 91
House bill
  cost of, 62, 75–76
  discussion of, 51
  passage of, 46, 54, 59–60
  proposal of, 48
  provisions of, 62–63
  Senate bill as compared to, 74
  statistics regarding, 99
House Education and Labor Committee, 54
House Energy and Commerce Committee, 54
House of Representatives
  Democratic Party seats in, 18, 23, 43
  negotiations in, 50, 53–54
  Republican Party seats in, 15
  Social Security legislation in, 18
  See also House bill
House Ways and Means Committee, 54
Hyde Amendment, 59

Idaho, lawsuit of, 118n10
implementation process of, 81–82
Indiana, lawsuit of, 118n10
Inflation Reduction Act, 92
Iowa, lawsuit of, 118n10

Jarrett, Valerie, 31–32
Johnson, Lyndon B., 2, 9, 11, 16–18
Joynt Kumar, Martha, 5. *See* Kumar, Martha Joynt

Kagan, Elena, 85
Kansas, lawsuit of, 118n10
Kennedy, Anthony, 85
Kennedy, Caroline, 41
Kennedy, Edward, 41
Kennedy, John F., 16, 17, 41
Kennedy, Joseph P., II, 66
Kennedy, Ted, 49, 57–58, 65–66
Kennedy, Vicki, 66
Kerry, John, 36
Kingdon, John, 7, 28
King v. Burwell, 89–90
Kirk, Paul G., Jr., 66
Korean War, 15
Kratovil, Frank, Jr., 76
Kucinich, Dennis, 78
Kumar, Martha Joynt, 5

Lambrew, Jeanne, 51
landmark decisions, 8–10
Landrieu, Mary, 61
Levin, Carl, 71
Lieberman, Joseph I., 61
Light, Paul C., 5
Louisiana, lawsuit of, 118n10

Maffei, Dan, 78
Magaziner, Ira, 20
Maine, lawsuit of, 118n10
Massachusetts, 48–49, 65–69, 96
McCain, John, 39, 43
McConnell, Mitch, 72
McDonnell, Bob, 70–71
McKinley, William, 102n6
Medicaid
  under ACA, 78–79, 82, 84, 85, 87, 91, 92, 97
  eligibility of, 89
  lessons from, 3
  origin of, 2, 16–18
Medicare
  under ACA, 78–79, 82, 85, 87
  donut hole of, 82
  lessons from, 3
  Medicare for all, 49
  opposition to, 18
  origin of, 2, 16–18
  prescription drug discounts for, 55

Medicare, *continued*
  reform considerations for, 62–63
Mendell, David, 36
Messina, Jim, 52
Michigan, lawsuit of, 118n10
Mills, Wilbur, 17–18
Mississippi, lawsuit of, 118n10

National Federation of Independent Business, 22
Nebraska, lawsuit of, 118n10
Nelson, Bill, 71
Neustadt, Richard E., 4, 6–7
Nevada, lawsuit of, 118n10
New York Public Interest Research Group, 30
New York Times (newspaper), 30, 35, 87–88, 91
New York Times Magazine, 39–40
Noonan, Peggy, 77
North Dakota, lawsuit of, 118n10

Obama, Barack
  accolades to, 31, 32, 41
  address to Congress by, 57–58
  on Affordable Care Act, 1, 60, 77, 79, 80, 81
  approval ratings for, 57
  background of, 27, 28–31
  on bipartisan summit, 72
  challenges of, 46
  on change, 43
  criticism of, 34
  decision-making process of, 6
  at Democratic National Convention, 35, 36
  Democratic presidential nomination win of, 39–42
  domestic policy agenda of, 7
  Dreams from My Father, 30
  education of, 28–30, 31
  on election, 5
  election of, 4–5, 40–41, 42–44
  goals of, 53
  on health care system/reform, 1, 26–27, 38, 45, 47, 50–51, 52, 53, 64–65, 70
  in Indonesia, 29
  influences on political views of, 28–31
  on law school, 31
  leadership assessment of, 2–3, 93–98
  legislative plan of, 58
  loss of, 34, 35
  on Massachusetts election, 69
  on Obamacare term, 86, 117n57
  policy announcement of, 57–58
  policymaking process of, 48–51, 95
  in politics, 32–37
  post-law school years of, 32
  on presidency, 8
  presidential candidacy of, 37–43, 86, 94
  Senate election of, 35–36, 37
  on single-payer system, 49
  on the Supreme Court, 84
  town hall meetings of, 56
  transformational leadership views on, 8
  transition of, 5–6, 43–44
  writings of, 32
Obama, Barack Hussein, Sr., 28
Obama, Malia, 34
Obama, Michelle Robinson, 31, 32, 35
Obama, Sasha, 34
Obamacare. *See* Affordable Care Act (ACA) (Patient Protection and Affordable Care Act)
Ohio, lawsuit of, 118n10

Partnership for Public Service, 5
passage components regarding, 7
Patient Protection and Affordable Care Act (ACA). *See* Affordable Care Act (ACA) (Patient Protection and Affordable Care Act)
Patrick, Deval, 66
Pelosi, Nancy, 73–74, 75, 77, 96–97
Pelosi, Paul, 73
Pennsylvania, lawsuit of, 118n10
Pfiffner, James P., 5, 6
Pharmaceutical Research and Manufacturers of America (PhRMA), 55
Plouffe, David, 41
Podesta, John, 43–44
polarization, 2, 9
policymaking, presidential leadership regarding, 6–7

politics, polarization in, 9
prescription drugs, discounts on, 55
presidents, leadership of, 3–8. *See also specific presidents*
Progressive movement, 13
Progressive Party, 13
Project Vote, 32

Rangel, Charles B., 54
Reagan, Ronald, 17
reconciliation budget process, 74–79, 96–97
Reid, Harry, 37–38, 61, 75
Republican Party
    bipartisan discussions of, 50–51
    election results of, 23
    government shutdowns of, 24
    health care reform discussion by, 60
    health care work of, 13
    Medicare opposition by, 18
    Obama's session with, 71
    voting statistics of, 59
Roberts, John, 85, 90
Rodham Clinton, Hillary. *See* Clinton, Hillary Rodham
Romney, Mitt, 39, 48–49, 86
Roosevelt, Franklin Delano, 13, 16, 102–103n6
Roosevelt, Theodore, 13
Rossiter, Clinton, 4
Rouse, Pete, 43–44
Rush, Bobby, 34, 35
Ryan, Paul, 63, 71

Sanders, Bernie, 92
Scalia, Antonin, 85
Schiliro, Philip M., 44, 52, 70, 89
Schilling, Curt, 67
Schlesinger, Arthur M., Jr., 4
Schlesinger, Arthur M., Sr., 4
Sebelius, Kathleen, 44, 51, 96
Senate
    Democratic Party seats in, 18, 23, 33, 43
    filibuster-proof majority loss in, 10, 65–69, 96, 109n68
    Obama in, 35–36, 37
    Republican Party seats in, 23, 33

    Social Security legislation in, 18
    transition confirmation in, 43
Senate bill
    bipartisan efforts regarding, 51
    concerns regarding, 76
    cost of, 62, 75–76
    discussion regarding, 49, 50, 60–62
    House bill as compared to, 74
    in the House, 75
    negotiations for, 55
    passage of, 46, 55, 62–63, 74, 77
    provisions of, 62–63
single-payer system, 49
Snowe, Olympia, 50, 61
socialism, 15
Socialist Party, 13
Social Security Act, 17–18
Soetoro, Lolo, 28
Sotomayor, Sonia, 85
South Carolina, lawsuit of, 118n10
South Dakota, lawsuit of, 118n10
Specter, Arlen, 109n68
State Children's Health Insurance Program (SCHIP), 24
states, refusals to enact ACA by, 87, 118n10
Stupak, Bart, 58–59
Stupak Amendment, 59, 76
Supreme Court, 84–85, 89–90
Supreme Court ruling of, 84–85, 89–90

Task Force on National Health Care Reform, 20–21
Tauzin, Billy, 55
taxation, 54, 59
Tax Cuts and Jobs Act, 90
technical difficulties regarding, 86–89
Texas, lawsuit of, 118n10
Thomas, Clarence, 85
Time (magazine), 40, 91–92
town hall meetings, 56
transactional leadership, 8
transformational leadership, 8
Tribe, Laurence H., 31
Truman, Bess, 18
Truman, Harry S., 2, 9, 11, 14–16
Trump, Donald, 90
Twenty-Second Amendment, 15

Utah, lawsuit of, 118n10

Virginia, lawsuit of, 118n10

Warner, Mark, 40
Washington, lawsuit of, 118n10
Washington Post (newspaper), 53
Waxman, Henry, 54

White House Care Interdepartmental Working Group, 20–21
Wilkins, David B., 31
Wisconsin, lawsuit of, 118n10
World War II, 14–15
Wyoming, lawsuit of, 118n10

Zients, Jeffrey D., 89

www.ingramcontent.com/pod-product-compliance
Lightning Source LLC
Chambersburg PA
CBHW030221170426
43194CB00007BA/814